BEAR TALES AND DEER TRAILS

BEAR TALES AND DEER TRAILS

by Mike McConnell

Writers Club Press
San Jose New York Lincoln Shanghai

Bear Tales and Deer Trails

All Rights Reserved © 2001 by Mike McConnell

No part of this book may be reproduced or transmitted in any form or by any means, graphic, electronic, or mechanical, including photocopying, recording, taping, or by any information storage retrieval system, without the permission in writing from the publisher.

Writers Club Press
an imprint of iUniverse, Inc.

For information address:
iUniverse, Inc.
5220 S. 16th St., Suite 200
Lincoln, NE 68512
www.iuniverse.com

ISBN: 0-595-21263-8

Printed in the United States of America

This book is for those who always dreamed of a life in the wild-wood. We did our best to live it for you.

Contents

Part I Bear Tales

NORTH TO ALASKA	3
FIRST BEAR	13
KINA COVE	17
SECOND WINTER	25
SALT CHUCK	41
LINDEMAN CREEK	51
MAD SOW	61
ELDEN'S BEAR	71
RICK'S BEAR	81
ACCIDENTAL BEAR	91
BACKYARD BEAR	99
CLOSE ENCOUNTERS	107

Part II DEER TRAILS

CHRISTMAS BUCK	117
LOST	127
BLACK POWDER	133
CONTENDER	137

SNOW BUCKS. 145
SUPERIOR 153
HARLEY 169
KING OF THE HILL. 175
THE RUT 183
PTARMIGAN MOUNTIAN. 201
WILDCAT 213
RAIN DEER 221
GUNS 231
Afterword 241

PART I

BEAR TALES

NORTH TO ALASKA

I was raised in a small Montana farming community a few miles from the confluence of the Missouri and Yellowstone rivers. It was a paradise for a kid obsessed with the outdoors. There was good fishing in both rivers, the hills were full of game to hunt and the area was ripe with frontier history. The Lewis and Clark expedition had split into two parts here to explore both rivers. Fort Union, a major military and fur trade post, was only fifteen miles up the Missouri from the mouth of the Yellowstone. The Custer Battlefield, Teddy Roosevelt's ranch, and the famous cow town of Miles City, were only a few hours drive from my home.

We hunted rabbits, pheasants, mule deer, whitetail deer, pronghorn antelope, and fished the rivers for catfish, sturgeon, and pike. I was also an avid reader and the literature of choice was tales of the fur trade, the cowboys, buffalo hunters, and mountain men. These heroes of the old west still loom larger than life in my imagination, so it's no wonder that I was drawn to Alaska as a young man.

During the early sixties I wandered out to Westport, a small fishing community on the Washington coast. I was walking on the dock one morning, looking at the boats and dreaming of adventure on the high seas. As I drifted along from boat to boat, a man who was working on fishing gear greeted me from the deck of a troller called the High C. I stopped and we fell into a conversation about one thing or another. He invited me aboard for coffee, and after visiting for a while asked me if I wanted a job as deckhand on the boat. I accepted without hesitation and we sailed for the fishing grounds off the coast of Oregon that evening. It was the beginning of what was to become my career for the next thirty years, and the planting of the seeds that would eventually take me to Southeast Alaska.

The skipper, Perry Coburn, was from Ketchikan and was married to a native woman from Kasaan Village on Prince Of Wales Island. I didn't know it at the time but Kasaan Bay would soon become the center around which some of the most exciting adventures of my life would develop.

We trolled for silver salmon off the mouth of the Columbia River for several weeks and in the fall I drifted back to Montana. It was several years before I made the break and headed north, but in early April of 1969 I finally arrived in Ketchikan on the Alaska State Ferry.

I was in Seattle in early February, hanging around the university district trying to figure out what to do with my life. I was working in a place called the U District Center, where we counseled drug addicts, draft dodgers, and ran a free food program for people with financial problems. Part of my job was to help people find a temporary place to sleep until their fortunes improved. One evening an interesting gentleman showed up at my desk, looking for a place to crash for the night. While I worked on finding him a place to sleep, he told me he was driving to Alaska up the Al-Can Highway. One thing led to another and I ended up going with him.

We headed north at daylight the next morning in an Austin Healy Sprite sports car with nothing but a couple sleeping bags lashed on the back and a gallon of cheap wine. We made it all the way to Whitehorse, Yukon before the money ran out. We split up there; my friend found a job and I hitchhiked back down the highway to McKenzie, BC where my sister lived. She was married to a Canadian who worked in a local sawmill. He got me on at the mill and I worked there till around the middle of April.

I still remembered the stories about Southeast Alaska that I had heard working on that troller. I could see no future at the mill and had no permit to work in Canada anyway, so I quit my job and bought a bus ticket to Prince Rupert. The Alaska State Ferry stopped there, and I soon found myself on the streets of Ketchikan. I had about twenty dollars in my pocket and no particular plan in mind.

I started hanging around the Yukon bar, crashing in a room upstairs and checking IDs for drinks at night. It was a pretty tough go with no money coming in and I eventually had to resort to the State Job Service Office. They found me a job out of Wrangell, working as a driller's helper on a core-drilling machine. It was a camp job and provided board and room and pretty good pay. I worked for several months until the job ended, then went back to Ketchikan. Summer was winding down and I needed to figure out something to do for the winter.

Earlier in the summer I had met Ron Arnce and John McKinley. They had invited me to come out to their place at Coal Bay, which happens to be in Kasaan Bay on Prince of Wales Island. Coal Bay is three miles across the bay from Kasaan Village, where Perry Coburn's wife was from!

I bought an old Russian army rifle at the local pawn shop, some winter clothes at Tongass Trading Co., and three boxes of groceries. When my shopping spree was finished, I hired Todd's Air Service to fly me out to Coal Bay that afternoon. After about a twenty-minute flight the little Cessna floatplane dropped me off on the beach in front of an old log house in the middle of nowhere. I knew I had found paradise!

During the early 1920's a fisherman named J. P. "Happy" Montplacier had built the big log house, which in those days was the showplace of the area. The house was about sixty feet long by forty feet wide, and was built out of twenty-four inch diameter red cedar logs. It had a steep roof made of hand split cedar shakes. The house sat on a point facing east, and had a spectacular view across Kasaan Bay toward the village.

Old Hap, as he was called, was married to a native woman named Nelly. After Hap died, in the early fifties, Nelly lived there by herself for several years, then moved to Ketchikan. She passed away a few years later and willed Coal Bay house to her niece, Joanne. Joanne was married to a nephew of Bob Arnce, Ron's father. Bob had been spending time at Coal Bay off and on since the late fifties. In the mid- sixties, Ron moved his family to Alaska and they made their home at Coal Bay. John McKinley and several other people spent most of their time there also, and the place became kind of a mountain man's commune. When I arrived in the fall of sixty-nine, there were about ten people living there. They made me welcome and I stayed for two years.

That first winter was quite an adventure. It snowed four feet in two days during late November, then turned cold over night and froze the bay solid. All the boats were frozen to the beach and buried in snow, and the firewood logs we had collected were also buried. The weather stayed clear and cold with a forty-knot north wind, and temperatures fell to around zero. In mid-December it warmed up to just below freezing and snowed three more feet. After that snowstorm the weather got clear, cold and windy and stayed that way till about the first of March.

It was pretty brutal. By the time Christmas rolled around, the grub was getting low and almost everyone had left for warmer climes. By early January there were only four of us left: Bob, his brother Rex, his youngest son, Rick, and myself. The ice in the bay was twelve inches thick. The nights were so cold water would freeze solid in the kitchen at night, even though the barrel stove was burning in the living room. We were down to beans, flour, coffee, and clams that we dug through the ice in front of the house at low tide. We had no cooking oil, no baking powder or yeast, and no sugar.

One day, Ed Todd circled the house in his floatplane. Bob fired a flare and Ed landed in the outer bay. The bay was frozen to about a half mile out in front of the house, so Ed taxied to the edge of the ice.

Bob and Rick grabbed their town clothes and went out across the ice to the plane. Their plan was go into Ketchikan, round up some grub and come back in a few days. We didn't see them again till late March, after the ice went out of the bay.

Rex and I subsisted on flour and water flapjacks fried in rancid oil skimmed off rotten mayonnaise out of the garbage, and beans with clams for dinner. Pretty grim fare, but after all, times like these are the essence of adventure and make good yarns in later years.

One cold, clear night in January, Rex and I were sitting in the living room after dinner. Rex was whittling on a piece of deer bone and I was reading. The dog, Cookie, was sleeping on the day bed near the door. It was a quiet, peaceful evening and we were a picture of contentment.

Suddenly, I heard a car drive up outside! The engine shut down and two doors slammed shut. I looked at Rex, who had a totally astonished look on his face. About that time Cookie went berserk and ran to the door, barking furiously. We leaped out of our chairs and ran to the front door. Outside we found a quiet starry night with no wind, and nothing else.

You have to understand that we were forty miles from the nearest road, frozen in a bay in the middle of nowhere. The sounds were so plainly that of a car driving up, the engine shutting down, and the doors slamming, that there was no doubt that is what we heard. We compared notes and our impressions were identical. Even the dog thought something, or someone, was outside.

I can't explain it; the air was very still and cold and perhaps the sound reflected off a layer of the atmosphere or something, who knows? The incident never happened again, but it sure left us spooked for the rest of the evening. Even the dog was nervous and took refuge in Rex's lap for the rest of the evening.

Our food supply became more and more limited as the weeks passed. We were really getting desperate for something to vary our diet. I remember one morning I was scrounging around in the shop and happened to open an old metal cupboard that we had moved out of the house during the fall. It had been used for food storage in the kitchen for several years and was in pretty tough shape. We had moved it to the shed to use as storage there.

The old cupboard was mostly empty, and the aluminum foil lining was still on the shelves. On the second shelf from the top was a treasure beyond imagining. There was an old jar of Grandma's Molasses lying on its side, and a puddle of molasses about four inches in diameter had formed under the leaky lid. The jar was empty, so I removed it carefully and tore out the section of aluminum foil that held the puddle of precious black fluid. I took my prize into the house, and Rex and I divided it carefully in half, then savored it slowly like the finest gourmet treat. We hadn't had anything even remotely sweet in over a month and it truly was delicious.

Interesting how a person will compromise convention in the face of adversity. Civilization is truly a thin veneer, and an empty belly has no sense of propriety whatsoever. If you are hungry enough you'll eat anything that even resembles food, and take as much delight in it as you would the best meal at the finest restaurant.

Sometime in early February we decided the situation called for drastic measures. We spent a day digging one of the skiffs out of the snow and chipping it loose from the ice. It was quite a project, but we eventually got it free and drug it out to the edge of the ice. Next morning, we launched the boat and rowed around to Kina Cove, which is the first inlet north of Coal Bay. We hoped to find a deer that the wolves had missed.

We spent the morning rowing along the shore on the north side of the cove, and eventually found one bedded down out of the wind on a sunny point. We chased it up and down the hill in deep snow for more than an hour, but never did get a shot at it. We were pretty disappointed and finally gave up, and headed for the house.

About one o'clock, as we rowed for home, Rex spotted a deer walking slowly along the beach on the point between Coal Bay and

Kina Cove. I got into the bow of the boat so I could take a rest with the rifle, and Rex rowed quietly toward the deer. When we were about twenty-five yards out, I shot it through the head. We were jubilant as we paddled in to claim our prize.

It was an old, spawned-out buck who had run off all his fat during the rut. The poor dilapidated critter was about as nearly starved to death as it could get and still be ambulatory. We could have cared less; it was the fatted calf to us.

We ate every morsel of that leathery old buck over the next several weeks. Rex made headcheese out of the head, and we boiled the feet with beans. It was amazing how that simple change in diet affected our sense of well being. We had been spending our days sitting in the living room doing nothing. We had even stopped talking for the most part. It wasn't that we were starving; we had food to eat every day, but no variety. I also suspect that there were vitamins and minerals in the meat, even in the poor condition that the deer was in, that we were not getting from our diet. In any case, we started doing things around the house that had been going wanting, and life definitely took a turn for the better.

One night in late February, the full moon came up over Kasaan Mountain to the east and turned the world into a wonderland of silvery light. The whole country lay buried under seven feet of snow, and the air was utterly clear. There were millions of ice crystals growing on every surface, and they reflected the moonlight like diamonds.

I had a venison dinner glowing under my belt and was feeling rather energetic, so I decided to take a walk. I bundled up in several layers of clothing, then headed out across the ice to the point between Coal Bay and Kina Cove. It was bitter cold, but the air was perfectly still. The moonlight reflecting off the snow and ice was so bright it was like a mystical kind of daylight. Everywhere you looked the light was refracting through the fans of ice crystals, which had a prismatic effect. There were jewels of red, green, and blue everywhere you looked. Overhead, the stars looked like diamonds shimmering in a silver-blue dome.

I walked around the point into Kina Cove and followed the south shore until I came to the ice. Kina Cove was also frozen from the head to a point about halfway out to the main bay. The ice here was also about twelve inches thick. I climbed over the jumble of ice cakes that the rising and lowering tide had broken up along the shoreline, then moved out onto the ice. The north wind had blown most of the snow off the frozen surface. Once I was out on the main sheet, it was easy walking.

The ice extended for about a half mile to the head of the bay. It was like being part of some surrealistic painting, as I walked along the smooth surface with the moon at my back. The surface of the ice was covered with beautiful fan-like frost crystals that crunched under my feet as I walked along. I almost felt guilty for the tracks I was leaving through the crystalline landscape.

I stopped in the middle of the bay and turned around slowly, drinking in the experience. Suddenly, over toward Coal Bay, the long eerie howl of a wolf echoed off the mountains at the head of the cove. It had hardly faded away when another wolf howled to the north. When that one ran out of breath, another near the head of the bay picked it up and added his notes to the mournful song.

The sound was a perfect, auditory complement to the visual wonder of the night. Without thinking, I threw back my head and cut loose with a howl of my own similar to the sound the wolves were making. As I ran out of breath and my voice faded, one of them added his call to mine. I stood there for about a half-hour, singing with them, each of us taking a turn, then another picking it up when the one singing ran out of breath.

As we sang, I could tell that they were moving. It dawned on me that they were hunting, and a sudden understanding flooded through me. They were scattered around the area. The sound of their howling served two purposes: they could keep track of each other, and it filled the deer with terror that started them moving on the hillsides. When a deer moved in the area where one of the wolves was, he would chase it. By howling, he could tell the rest of the pack that he was in pursuit, and in which direction the deer was moving. They could then set up an ambush to trap the deer as it was driven through the pack.

I stopped howling and listened to them. I could follow the hunt that gradually seemed to move over toward the house. I walked back around the point, hoping to keep up with them. The pack seemed to concentrate in back of the house, over in the head of the south arm of the bay. I stopped at the house and coaxed Rex out to listen.

We crept through the woods behind the house and came out on the beach, about half way up the south arm. Right across from us we could hear them snarling and the sound of bones cracking. It was a frightening sound; it made the hair stand up on the back of my neck! I had an overpowering urge to go back to the house and mind my own business. We stayed for about ten minutes, listening to the feeding frenzy across the narrow strip of ice, then headed for the house.

In the morning we went back for a closer look and found nothing but a bloody spot in the snow just inside the trees. There was little left of the deer, just the jawbone and a circle of hair about ten feet in diameter. We followed the tracks for some distance until they headed off towards Ives Lake. As near as we could tell, there were about six wolves in the pack. We found several other kills that winter, but this was the only time we got to participate. It was a memorable night. I will never forget the sound of those bones crunching.

FIRST BEAR

Ron, his wife and daughters, and Bob and Rick had been home for a few days. After the months of frozen solitude, the old house was filled with life and our diet had improved considerably.

During the winter, the subject of bears and bear hunting had come up many times. None of us had much realistic information about bears and how to hunt them. There was a strange mystique that surrounded the notion of hunting an animal that had the ability to fight back. By spring it had taken on the attributes of a rite of passage, an initiation into the realm of the true hunter. The willingness to walk up to an animal that has the ability to kill you, and put a bullet into it, to kill or be killed, must certainly put you in the same league with men like Dan Boon, Jim Bridger, and Jeremiah Johnson. Anyway, by spring I figured I was ready.

We saw the first bear on the 29th of March. The bear appeared on the beach south of the house for a few minutes, then disappeared into the woods. It caused quite a stir and much oiling of guns and sharpening of knives.

A few days later, one of Ron's girls came racing into the house shouting that there was a bear on the beach in the west arm of the bay! Rex decided that he was going to shoot it, so he and Bob loaded their rifles and slipped into the woods behind the house to begin the stalk. About twenty minutes later we heard a shot and went out on the beach to see if they had made meat. Sure enough, Rex had killed a nice young male with a neck shot from about fifty yards. The place was a buzz of excitement. We all went to help load it in the skiff and bring it back to the house. We hung the bear in the shop and Rex skinned it out carefully. The weather was warming and we had no refrigeration, so we enjoyed some of the meat fresh and canned the rest.

Meanwhile, Rex worked on the hide. He cleaned off all the fat and other tissue, then tanned it in a salt brine with oxalic acid added to set the hair. It came out pretty good, considering our lack of experience.

June rolled around, the snow was finally gone, and the sedge grass was knee-high along the beaches. I had seen several bears over the weeks, but had been unable to approach one close enough for a shot. Finally, one gray, overcast, drizzly morning, Rex spotted one on the south beach near the mouth of Ives Creek. We were having our morning coffee and Rex could see it out the window from his chair. The bear was in a spot that was easy to approach through the woods, and the wind was in the east; perfect for a stalk. I decided it was time for me to do it, and Ron was willing to back me up.

I had been tinkering on an old J.C. Higgens 30-06 that someone had left there the summer before. I knew it was sighted in to put a 220-grain bullet on point of aim at 100 yards. I loaded it with Remington Core-Locked factory loads, then Ron and I slipped quietly out the back door. The rest of the gang had front row seats out the living room windows.

Coal Bay has two arms, one to the southwest and one to the northwest. The old log house sits on the point between the two arms. We cut through the woods west of the house, then crossed the tide flat at the head of the southwest arm of the bay. The forest was fairly open along that side of the bay, so we went into the timber, then followed the well-used game trail just inside the trees.

As we worked our way carefully toward the little cove where the bear was feeding, my heart was pounding and my mouth was dry. My mind jumped from one worry to another as we moved slowly toward the bear. "Would the bear still be there? Is the rifle really sighted in right? Will I shoot poorly and wound him?" etc., etc.

It took about ten minutes to reach a clump of alders across the creek from the bear. He was standing belly-deep in the sedge grass, halfway between the creek and the woods, his fur blue-black against the green of the tall grass. We wiggled into the alders, and I found a branch that was the right height off the ground to make a perfect rifle rest. I sat on the ground with the rifle on the branch, and rested my right elbow on my knee. It made a dead-steady rest with a clear view of the bear over the sights.

I looked over at Ron. He had found a good spot a few feet to my left. He nodded that he was ready, and I saw him ear back the hammer on his Winchester 30-30. I looked back at the bear. He was quartering up the beach with his rump to my right and his head to the left. He was eating grass and would reach down, take a mouthful, and then raise his head to look around while he chewed. I took a sight picture on his body behind the near front leg.

A strange coolness settled over me. My heartbeat and breathing had settled into an easy rhythm. My mind was totally focused on the bear; it was like looking down a tunnel toward him. I watched him over the rifle sights, and gradually took up the slack in the trigger. I noticed that when he reached down to take a bite of grass, his head would stop moving for four or five seconds. I moved the front bead to his neck, right where it connects to the back of the skull, but by the time I got a sight picture he raised his head. I held the sight on the place where his neck joint had been, and when he lowered his head for more grass, the spot reappeared in the sights.

KAA-BOOOOMMMM-OOMMM-WOMMmmm.........The rifle fired magically by itself, and the muzzle blast echoed off the hills. The last thing I saw was a mist of water spray into the air, then the rifle recoiled. "All right! Good shot!" Ron shouted, punching me on the shoulder and got to his feet. I bolted another cartridge into the rifle, put on the safety, and got to my feet. My knees felt weak and my heart was pounding again as we walked slowly across the creek and up the beach toward the bear.

As we approached the black hump in the grass, I noticed that the seat of my pants was soaked from sitting on the wet ground and my legs were trembling. We walked up to the bear, and while I pointed my rifle at the head, Ron poked him with his gun barrel.

"He looks pretty dead to me," Ron said, grinning at me. I grinned back, trying to think of something cool to say, but I was pretty stunned by the enormity of the moment. I heard the outboard motor fire up over at the house and in a few minutes Rex, Bob, and Rick arrived with the skiff. When they were ashore, they congratulated me enthusiastically and I told the whole story in graphic detail.

"Well, the fun is over; now the work starts," Bob said, taking the critter by the hind leg and turning him over on his back. We field-dressed the bear, then wrestled the carcass into the boat. Back at the house, we carried him up to the shed and hung him inside. Breakfast was ready, so we decided to eat before we skinned it. I was so excited I could hardly eat.

After breakfast Rex helped me skin my prize. The bear was a fully mature male in prime condition, and he still had some winter fat left from the fall before. The bullet had hit right where I was aiming. It smashed the first vertebrae below the skull. It had killed him instantly and he still had the last bite of grass in his mouth.

Due to the late spring, the hide was still prime. Usually they are getting somewhat rubbed out by early June, but the pelt turned out good and I had it for many years. It was a grand adventure shared with good friends. That first year at Coal Bay was the beginning of a lifelong fascination with bears, bear hunting, and bear guns. There were hard lessons ahead, but the experience of learning them is what makes life interesting.

KINA COVE

It was mid-September and we had developed a hunger for some fresh deer meat. The season had opened on August first, but the deer usually stayed in the alpine meadows until the first frosts of fall pushed them to lower elevations. There is some special quality about the autumn air that always stirs up my hunting instincts. As the days get shorter, and the berry bushes start turning yellow, I get this itch that must be scratched. I need to be sneaking along some cedar ridge with the weight of a rifle in my hand, and the heady smell of fall muskeg in my nose.

One cool, clear afternoon, the urge finally overcame inertia. I took the 'ought six down off its pegs on the log ceiling beam in the living room, and headed out the door. Rex raised an eyebrow as I passed his chair, but said nothing. I walked down the beach toward the head of the northwest arm of Coal Bay. The trail to Kina Cove started there and that seemed to be where I was inclined to go.

Kina Cove is the next bay north of Coal Bay. The trail comes out on the south shore of Kina Cove, about a quarter mile from the head of the bay. It was about a twenty-minute walk through open muskeg with a fringe of timber on both ends. The valley at the head of the cove had been logged during the mid-1950's, and the old logging roads on either side of the creek made for easy access up the valley. Deer frequented the area in the fall, and I figured it would be as good a place to start as any.

There were runs of pink and dog salmon that spawned in Kina Creek every fall. The runs were about over for the year, but when I came out on the beach I could see some late bloomers splashing in the mouth of the creek. As I walked toward the stream, a couple bedraggled looking bald eagles flapped tiredly into the air and glided into the top of a lone hemlock tree that the loggers had left behind.

There were fish carcasses in various stages of decomposition strewn about the banks, and the creek was full of the dead and dying. The air reeked of rotten fish, wet birds, and bear crap. I crossed quickly and pushed my way into the dense tangle of alder brush that choked the old logging road on the north side of the creek.

The bears had a well-used trail up the road through the alders, and I followed it up the hill. After a short climb, the brush thinned out and the going became easier. The road angled up the valley away from the creek, gradually climbing the north ridge.

The clear-cut on both sides was a nearly impenetrable tangle of berry bushes, devil's club, and a few small spruce and hemlock saplings. Game trails occasionally crossed the road and there were old deer tracks, but nothing very fresh. About a half mile from the beach, the creek makes a bend toward the south side of the valley. The road climbs the hill on the north side to the top of a bluff. The hillside is steep, and you can't see the creek from the road.

I finally found a set of fresh deer tracks on top of the hill. I decided to sit behind a bush above the road for a while. It was getting on toward evening, and I figured there was a good chance that the critter would walk past my ambush spot before dark, so I settled down to wait.

I had a nice view across the valley and the fall colors were magnificent in the evening light. I could hear salmon splashing in the creek, and a pair of ravens were performing aerobatics in the air currents. They would glide along, then one of them would make a peculiar croaking noise that sounded like water dripping in a barrel. At the end of the call he would fold his wings and do a complete roll. The ravens always seem to be having a good time and never appear to take life very seriously.

I was sitting with my back against a stump, with the rifle resting in the crook of my left arm. I was being very still, enjoying the view, daydreaming about one thing or another. Across the valley I could see the other logging road that angled up the mountain behind Coal Bay. I chuckled to myself as the memory of a rotten night that Rick and I had endured on that road about a year ago flashed into my mind.

It was late September and we were enjoying a spell of Indian summer. Rick and I were bored and craving action, so we decided to go camp out in Kina Cove and sample the trout fishing in the creek. We loaded ourselves up with equipment like two pack mules, and headed out about noon. After an exhausting afternoon of humping through the muskeg, then up the road on the south side of the Kina Creek, we finally made a simple camp in the middle of the old logging road. We had an army poncho and a scrap of visqueen for shelter, and a wool blanket and an old sleeping bag for a bed.

When the camp was complete, we climbed down to the stream and actually did manage to catch a few small cutthroat trout. For bait we used eggs out of a female pink salmon that Rick snagged out of the creek. The trout were not very big, but we weren't particular and we soon had enough for dinner. We fried them up in the ten-inch cast iron skillet that we had packed over from the house.

We sat cross-legged by our fire in the last rays of the evening sun, munching trout in front of our shelter in the wilderness. We felt a kinship with all the hunters, trappers, and explorers who had gone before us. Livin' off the land, wild free souls who weren't dependent upon civilization, who lived by their own law and by their own wits. At least that's how the evening started. Unfortunately, we were about to get a dose of Mother Nature in the raw.

We sat yarnin' around the fire until about nine o'clock, then crawled under the shelter and turned in for the night. Our bellies were full and we were glowing with self-satisfaction. It wasn't long before we were snoring away, dreaming of golden-brown trout sizzling in a cast iron skillet over a cedar fire. As I lay there grinning contentedly in my sleep, the sizzling got louder and louder until it finally woke me out of my slumber.

What I was really hearing was the sound of rain drops the size of golf balls splattering into the few remaining coals of our fire. I could also hear the wind in the trees on the hill above us. In a moment the shelter started to flap in the wet wind that came blowing up the creek. Within a few minutes the shelter was whipping like crazy and rain was flogging down so hard that the fire was soon a steaming memory. Then it rained harder. We did okay for a while; the tarp was flapping and rain was blowing in, but we still had some shelter from the deluge that was pounding down outside.

Our camp was on a small, flat spot in the road at the foot of a hill. When the logging crew had built the road they had put a culvert in to allow the small stream that came off the hill to continue on down to the main creek. Trouble was, the culvert had long since silted in and was too small to carry the volume of water falling out of the sky that night. Mother Nature, in her wisdom, wasn't one to let that stop her, so she simply diverted part of the creek down the road when the culvert got too full to handle the load.

By midnight, there was nothing left of our tarps but a few ragged flaps. We were lying in a stream of muddy water about two inches deep. We were as totally soaked as we could get and getting wetter. The night was absolutely pitch-black dark and we had no flashlight, so all we could do was lay there in our soggy blankets and suffer.

I have enjoyed some miserable nights since, but none to even remotely compare to that one. As the night progressed, the water running down the road got deeper, and we eventually had to sit up to keep from drowning in the four-inch deep river we were lying in. We finally crawled to the edge of the road and climbed the bank to get out of the water.

We sat huddled together in our wet blankets until the first pale-gray streaks of dawn finally started to glow in the east. When we could see to travel, we abandoned our gear and took off for the house. We went back two days later, after the storm passed, and packed our rigging home.

The rest of the gang put forth a heroic effort to not rib us too much, but it was more than they could stand. References to our camping trip came up in every story session for the rest of the winter. Those trout were pretty tasty, though!

The images of the past slowly faded, and my attention returned to the present. Suddenly there was a flicker of movement to my left. I slowly turned just my eyes to look. A sparrow had landed on the rifle barrel about an inch from the front sight. As I watched in amazement, it began preening, smoothing each wing-feather with its beak and then combing its breast. When it was finished, it fluffed up and put its head under its wing and went to sleep.

I didn't quite know what to do. I was sitting there, intending to kill the deer if it walked by, and this little guy had settled in for the night on my gun barrel! I thought about just chasing him away but couldn't bring myself to do it. He looked so comfortable perched there. A few minutes later the problem solved itself.

Suddenly, from down on the creek, there was a tremendous bellowing roar! It was followed by a series of loud grunts and then a piercing scream. I jumped about a foot and the sparrow vanished. There were more screams and splashing sounds. All the birds were in the air, adding to the racket, and it sounded as every fish in the stream was in motion.

I stood up to see what was happening. I couldn't actually see the creek from the road because of the brush, so I decided to try to get closer. I scrambled down the bank off the road, then pushed my way through the brush toward the creek. As I fought my way through the tangle I could hear snarling, splashing, and an occasional bloodcurdling scream. The scream made the hair stand up on my neck. It sounded like someone was being murdered down there.

I pushed out into a tiny opening, and climbed up on an old stump that gave me a view of the creek. There was a mature bear chasing a smaller one back and forth across the stream. After a few bounds, the small bear would stop and turn to fight. The big one would pounce on it and the fur would fly! After a couple seconds the little bear would break free and run away.

While these two were going at it, the terrible shrieking started again off to my left. About fifty yards downstream, there were two cubs in a small sapling. The tree was only about twenty feet high and was bending toward the ground with their weight. The sow was huffing and snorting as she paced back and forth at the base of the tree, and the cubs were screaming at the top of their lungs.

As I looked around, I realized there were several more bears scattered along the section of creek that was visible from my perch. I counted seven altogether. The two that were fighting would separate for a few minutes then go at it again. The other two seemed to be mostly uninterested in the altercation. Once in a while one would look up from his fishing and watch for a few seconds, but the lure of food would soon draw their attention back to the creek.

The sow eventually let the cubs come down out of the tree, and they disappeared downstream. The birds came back a few at a time, and by the end of an hour a truce seemed to have been negotiated. Everyone was busy with their evening feed.

It was getting on toward dark, so I climbed back up to the road and headed for home. I never did see a deer, but I collected another adventure that I have enjoyed relating over the years whenever the subject of bears is being discussed. I also gained a healthy respect for the potential danger of messing around with wild animals. Watching those bears fight and that old sow protecting her cubs made me realize they were not to be taken lightly. Without a gun, a person

•

wouldn't stand much of a chance if he accidentally provoked one of them to fight.

SECOND WINTER

The fall turned into winter and we were soon buried in snow again. Ron and his family had moved to Ketchikan permanently during the summer. Bob and Rick soon followed. The bay was frozen solid to the outer points by late November, and it looked as we were in for another brutally cold season.

Three other would-be mountain men wintered with Rex and me that year. Dave, we had met one afternoon in July. Ron's wife, Gail, and another woman had taken their laundry up to the creek in the west arm of the bay. They had been gone about a half-hour when we heard one of them scream. Ron and I grabbed our rifles off the wall and ran out of the house thinking they had seen a bear. When we got there we found them talking to a tall, bearded man in ragged clothes. They introduced him as Dave and said he had walked across the peninsula from Skowl Arm.

We were impressed; we had studied the route on topographical maps, thinking about trying it ourselves sometime. It was about five miles as the crow flies. You follow Cabin Creek to a large lake, walk along the east shore of the lake to an unnamed stream, then up over a low pass and down the drainage into Coal Bay. No small feat.

We took him to the house and fed him breakfast. While he ate, he told us his story. He was from New Orleans and had come to Ketchikan in the spring looking for some real wilderness. He wanted to build a cabin and spend a winter in it. He bought a twelve-foot plywood rowboat and a .270 rifle and rowed north out of Ketchikan in

May. When he came out of Tongass Narrows, he turned west across Clarence Strait toward Kasaan Bay and ended up in McKenzie Inlet in Skowl Arm.

It was a bold crossing in that tiny boat; it's about fifteen miles across Clarence Strait, and it is one of the meanest pieces of water in the world. He said it had taken him fifteen hours to cross from Vallenar Point to Grindall Island, and that the water had been calm. Anyway, he had landed at the mouth of Old Tom's Creek and was building a cabin. He had heard about Coal Bay and decided to come pay us a visit for a few days. He had rowed his boat to the mouth of Cabin Creek and stashed it in the edge of the timber. He had a good topographical map of the peninsula between Skowl Arm and Kasaan Bay, and had made the walk over in about twelve hours. Dave stayed for a few days and we eventually ran him home in Ron's skiff. That was the last we saw of him until late October.

One evening, just as we were finishing dinner, we heard a shout out on the beach. It was dark, so Rex grabbed a flashlight and we walked down the trail to the boat landing. There was Dave in his rowboat piled full of all his worldly belongings. He said the Forest Service had run him out of his shack and he needed a place to winter. We had lots of room, so we invited him to stay. He was a good man and we enjoyed having him there.

Deer season was in full swing and we were doing a lot of hunting. Dave had never killed a deer, so he was full of questions and went out almost every day. One afternoon, he had been around the south point in Little Coal Bay, and had decided to cut across the point into the home bay.

He was walking along through a muskeg, humming to himself, and decided to try to play a tune on his deer call. He really got into it and was sort of dancing along the trail, tweetling away on the call. He saw a movement out of the corner of his eye, and turned to find two does following along with him, listening intently to the music. Not being one to pass up an opportunity like that, he raised his rifle and shot one of them. The other one hung around while he gutted its partner, then followed him to the beach as he carried out the dead one. Naturally we all tried his deer calling technique, but nobody else could make it work.

The incident reminded me of an occurrence that had happened during the previous summer. The Fourth of July was getting close, and we had invited a bunch of people out from town to celebrate. One of the things we wanted to do was try to roast a whole deer on a spit. We had been hunting hard, and as the big day drew near we still hadn't found one to shoot.

By the morning of the third, we had just about given up on the idea. It was a nice sunny morning, and Bob had wandered out on the beach south of the house to warm his bones in the morning sun. He found a gravel beach up the south arm of the bay, and was sitting in the sun enjoying the fine summer morning.

He usually carried a harmonica in his pocket, and he suddenly had an urge to play a tune or two. He took out the harp and whittled out a few variations on Turkey In The Straw. When he stopped for breath, he looked up and saw two little spike bucks standing about twenty yards down the beach, looking curiously at him. Unfortunately, he had left his gun at the house. He played several notes on the harmonica and the two deer took a few steps closer. Bob stood up slowly and started for the house, bending a few notes on the mouth harp. The deer followed like rats following the Pied Piper of Hamlin.

They followed him all the way to the trail up into the yard. Bob went in the house and grabbed his Marlin off the wall, then stalked carefully out onto the outhouse boardwalk. The two little bucks were standing on the beach, looking up the trail toward the house. In the twinkling of an eye, we had our deer for the party. The barbecue was a success and a good time was had by all, thanks to Bob's musical talents.

Dave had a sort of innocent magic about him when it came to hunting deer. I don't know if it was beginner's luck or what, but that fall he seemed to be the only one that could find a deer. One morning, just before the big snow came, he rowed across the bay and burrowed his way into one of the worst tangles of brush in the area. We all avoided the place because the underbrush was so thick in some places you had to crawl on your hands and knees along the bear trails.

About mid-morning, we heard a shot, and sometime later he came up the trail to the house. He said he had killed a big buck over on the point and it was too heavy to carry; he needed some help. A couple of us went back with him and he lead us on a merry scramble through some horrible country.

Eventually, we came out in a small muskeg that I had never seen before. He figured the deer was around there somewhere, but he couldn't remember exactly where. We circled around for about an hour, and finally found the deer in another muskeg. It wasn't even connected to the one where he thought he had left the buck. We ended up taking it out on the beach in Kina Cove and walking back around the point to get the skiff to bring it home.

During November, there was a set of very low tides, so we decided to go clam digging. There was a reef that bared on a minus tide about a hundred yards off the point between Coal Bay and Kina Cove. It was excellent clam country and our plan was to go out and dig a wash tub full and re-bury them on the beach in front of the house. That way we could have clams anytime without having to go out in the boat.

Low tide was about eight o'clock at night, well after dark. After supper, we loaded the shovels and tubs into the skiff, then idled out to the reef. We beached the boat on the south side of the reef and walked across to the north side to dig. After I had dug for a while I got bored and decided to walk around the reef to see if I could find a better bed of clams. I gradually worked my way clear around to the south side where we had anchored the skiff. It was gone! I shone my flashlight out into the darkness and could just barely see it floating about fifty yards off the shore.

I couldn't swim a stroke, so I took off for the other side of the reef as fast as I could go. When I was about fifty yards from the pool of lantern light where the other men were working, I yelled, "THE BOAT IS LOOSE AND I CAN'T SWIM!"

"OKAY; WE'RE GETTING THEM HERE, TOO," someone yelled back.

"NO, NO, THE @#$% BOAT IS LOOSE! IT'S GETTING AWAY!" I hollered again. There was a short pregnant silence, then I heard somebody say, "oh shit," and they all jumped up and came running. When we got to the spot where the skiff had been anchored, you could just barely make it out in the beam of a flashlight.

Without a word, Dave shoved his flashlight in his hip pocket with the switch still on, and plunged into the icy cold water. He never even took off his boots. He had on a heavy wool coat, wool pants, and high-top rubber boots. We could hear him splashing and gasping and he was soon out of sight, except for the flashlight glowing dimly in the water. Eventually we heard something bump the side of the boat. We could hear him grunting and banging around and see the light flashing occasionally.

"I'M AT THE BOAT, BUT I CAN'T GET IN!" he yelled between gasping breaths.

"GO AROUND TO THE STERN AND CLIMB UP THE MOTOR," someone yelled back. We heard more grunting and banging.

"OKAY, I'M IN THE BOAT BUT I DON'T KNOW HOW TO START THE OUTBOARD," he yelled.

"USE THE OARS," I yelled back. We heard more clunking around, then the splash of the oars. In a few moments, we could see the ghost-like shape of the boat coming into the circle of light cast by the two Coleman lanterns we were holding.

When the bow of the skiff touched the shore, we could see that Dave was exhausted and shivering. We gathered up our gear, piled in the boat, and took off for the house.

There is no doubt that Dave saved our lives; we were over a hundred yards from the mainland and about two miles from the house. Dave was the only one that could swim, and he doubted that he could have made it to the shore. He said he barely had the strength to climb aboard when he got to the boat.

The glow of the kerosene lamps shining in the living room windows was a welcome sight as we rounded the point and motored toward the house. What happened? We forgot to put out the anchor in our eagerness to start digging, and as the tide came in the boat just floated away.

The next deer Dave got was after the big freeze. The bay was frozen clear to the outer points and the ice was about a foot thick. There was also about four feet of snow, which made hunting just about impossible. One morning Dave decided to walk across the ice and go around into Kina Cove. We watched out the front room windows as he crossed the ice and disappeared behind the point. A few minutes later, we saw him come back around the point carrying something on his back. Rex took the binoculars off their hook between the windows and looked across the frozen bay. Dave was just climbing across the broken ice slabs that littered the beach.

"It's a deer, but it's weird. It looks like it's still alive," he said, handing me the binoculars. I looked and sure enough, he had a deer across his shoulders, but it had its head up looking toward me. As he neared the house we could soon see that the deer was frozen solid. We figured that the wolves had chased it into the water, and when it had climbed out it was so exhausted that it lay down on the beach and froze to death.

We speculated at some length about whether the deer was fit to eat ' or not, and finally decided to give it a try. Dave and Rex tried to skin the carcass, but the hide was frozen solid to the meat. They discussed trying to thaw it out in the house, but decided that it would take several days to thaw all the way through and would probably spoil when it warmed up. They finally hacked off a front shoulder with an ax and thawed it out enough in the oven to get the hide off. They roasted it up, and it wasn't bad if you didn't mind picking a few hairs out of your gravy.

The next day, they discovered the handsaw method of butchering frozen meat. They sawed steaks out of a hindquarter. Each one was a cross-section of the ham, including the bone, meat and hide. The skin peeled off while the meat was frozen and generally it worked pretty well. When the hindquarters were gone, they continued to saw cross-sections out of the back. They were quite educational. Each one was a section through the whole deer, about an inch thick. You could see the back straps, the hide, the belly walls, the guts, and the stomach. We managed to eat most of it, but it always seemed to me to taste like the guts smell when you are field-dressing a carcass.

Another interesting character that wintered with us that year was a kid named Mark. He had turned up in the summer with some other people who had stopped by for a visit. He was so taken with the place that he had stayed.

Mark was from California and had grown up in the city. He was about the most mechanically helpless person I ever met. We had a new outboard motor that fall and Mark never could get it to start. All you had to do was pull out the choke, give it a little throttle, and yank the starting rope once, but try as he might, it wouldn't start for him. Even the oars defied him; when he tried to row one of the skiffs he looked like a drunken spider. One thing he could do, though, was play the guitar. He had been a music teacher in real life and we had many hours of enjoyment from his playing that winter.

There was a small beaver pond south of the house called Ives Lake. Mark had a thing about that lake and was always talking about building a cabin there. One warm fall day he decided to go get started on the project. He set out for the lake loaded down with enough equipment to supply a small army and we didn't see him again for two days. One morning, someone saw him limp out of the woods without his gear, using a stick for a crutch. Dave went over and picked him up in the skiff and brought him to the house. Mark had a deep gash in the instep of his foot and quite a tale to tell.

It seems that when he arrived at the lake, he was a bit over-heated from humping his big backpack full of equipment up through the woods. After unpacking some of his gear, he decided to take a dip in the lake to cool off. When he climbed out of the water, he stepped on a sharp twig that caused him to stagger and step on the bit of his ax, which was leaning against a small tree. He lurched away from the ax, knocking his old Winchester 30-30 over. For some reason known only to Mark, the rifle had a round in the chamber and the hammer was on full cock. Lucky for him it fell with the muzzle pointing away from him, because it fired.

The bullet hit a 30-caliber ammo can that contained his matches, candles, first aid kit, and a box of cartridges for the rifle. When the bullet passed through the can, the matches lit up and started a fire that spread instantly to the candles. The lid was cracked just enough to give the fire enough oxygen to really burn. Mark was busy with his cut foot and didn't notice the fire until 30-30 shells started to cook off. Only a couple cartridges went off, and the bullets didn't penetrate the metal can, but he lost all of his matches and his first aid kit.

So there he was; a mile off the beach with a really bad cut on his foot, nothing to bandage it with, and no way to make a fire. He cleaned up the foot as best he could, and bandaged it with his tee shirt. He fired three shot distress signals with the rifle until he ran out of shells, but we never heard them at the house. He was behind a hill and the wind was in the north. After a cold, painful night he found a stick for a crutch and hobbled out to the beach.

Come winter, Mark's foot had healed up, but he was still obsessed with Ives Lake. In January, we were getting low on grub again and had long since eaten up all the meat we had canned during the fall.

One day Mark took the notion that he was going to go to the lake and catch us a mess of trout by fishing through the ice. We tried to explain that there wasn't enough food value in all the trout in the lake to replace the energy he would burn. He would have to force his way to the lake through four feet of snow, then chop through the ice. He had his mindset though, so he took off in the morning with his big backpack full of camping gear and a pair of old snowshoes on his feet.

He showed up back at the house about noon the next day, worn down to a nub and with no trout to show for his efforts. He said it took him about three hours to get to the lake. The snowshoes were too big for the heavy underbrush, and the binding had come apart about halfway to the lake. He had gone on without them in waist-deep snow, and when he arrived at the lake the snow was even deeper.

He rested for a while, then made camp. When he had a snow cave dug with some bows for a roof, he went to the lake with his shovel and ax to cut a hole in the ice. The snow was five feet deep and it took quite a while to dig down to the ice. When he finally had a place dug out big enough to work in, he started chopping at the ice with his ax. It was tough going, and the ice was thicker than he had expected. In fact, after an hour of chopping and shoveling out the chips, it wasn't water he found it was frozen mud. The lake was frozen clear to the bottom!

Well, Mark was no quitter, you had to give him that. He climbed out of the pit, moved his operation farther out in the middle of the lake, and started again. The wind had blown some of the snow off the ice, so he only had to clear out about two feet of it to get down to the ice. The ice here was clear and black and he was sure he could see water through it. He whacked away with the ax for a while, but as luck would have it, just before he broke through, the ax handle broke right behind the head. He tried chipping with just the head for a while, but the hole was so deep that he knew it would take forever with no handle in the ax.

Necessity, however, as we all know, is the mother of invention. He went back to camp and got the old Winchester. It only took about five shots before water started to seep into the hole. Trouble was, he had a cone-shaped pit about three feet deep, with a .30 caliber hole in the bottom. The excavation was soon full of water. The tiny bullet hole was too small to fish through and he had no way to widen the hole. There was pressure under the ice from the weight of the snow and the water soon overflowed the top to the hole, and started to spread on top of the ice.

Mark grabbed his tools and headed for the shore. It was about dark, so he went back to his cave and crawled into his sleeping bag to wait out the long, winter night. In the morning, he packed up his gear and slogged home. Every once in a while he would talk about going back for another try, but he never quite got around to it.

The old log house at Coal Bay was pretty hard to heat; all we had for firewood was red cedar, which didn't put out many BTUs. The floor was always cold and Rex had a hard time keeping his feet warm. He was kind of an inventor, and was always working on one crackpot scheme or another. One day he got the bright idea that since deer hair was hollow, it should make great insulation. We had a lot of it around that we had scraped off several deer hides we were tanning. Rex took his two best pairs of wool socks and put one inside the other. Next he packed a layer of loose hair between them, and sewed through them from the inside out so the deer hair would stay in place and not bunch up.

It took him several days of fiddling around to perfect the idea, but he eventually had a pair of thick, quilted, insulated socks. He wore them around the house for the afternoon and evening and declared the project a success. He was so pleased with them that the next morning he decided to take a walk and try them in the great outdoors. The ultimate test, as it were.

He was gone about two hours, and when he came back he was limping like he had rocks in both boots. His face was red, and when I asked what was wrong with his feet, he just said, "harumph," and headed for his chair in the living room. He kicked off his rubber boots and yanked the socks off as quickly as he could. It seems that things had gone okay for a while. Eventually, however, the stiff hairs had worked through the weave of the socks, and the tips had started poking him in the feet like hundreds of stickers. It was really cold out and he had little choice but to hotfoot it back to the house.

By the time he got home he was in agony. He said it felt like the socks were full of porcupine quills. Another good idea that didn't pan out. He spent the next two days picking the hairs out of his best socks and grumbling about the wasted effort. The rest of us kind of avoided the issue.

Just before Christmas, Rex decided he was going into town. He hadn't been in for about eighteen months and he figured he better go make sure he could still navigate in civilization. We all threw what money we had in the pot and gave him a list of things we wanted. Most of it would go for food, but there would be enough for a box of rifle shells here, or a new pocketknife there. We also needed sandpaper, steel wool, a couple files, and other hardware items.

One morning we heard a plane overhead and I went out and fired a 12-gauge flare at it. The pilot saw the flare, circled around and landed. He taxied up to the edge of the ice and waited for us to come out to meet him. By that time, Rex had his town kit together and he hurried out to the plane and climbed aboard. Moments later, the plane took off and life returned to normal around the house.

As the days went by we all savored the excitement of the prospects of some town food to eat and the small treasures we had ordered. More days passed and it seemed, as though Rex should have been back. We had no communication with town, so all we could do was wait. More days passed and Christmas was getting closer every day.

Finally, on the day before Christmas Eve, we heard a plane circle the house. In a few minutes it landed and taxied to the edge of the ice. We all walked out to help pack the loot to the house, and as we approached the edge of the ice, we could see that Rex had brought someone with him. The plane taxied away before we got there, and as I approached, I noticed that there wasn't much luggage on the ice with Rex and the other person.

As I walked up to them, I could tell right away that they had had a few drinks. The other person was a woman, and she was hanging on his arm like a cheap suit. All they had with them was a couple duffel bags and one small box. They greeted us effusively and we walked back to the house in silence.

When we were in our chairs in the living room, someone finally asked where the grub and hardware items were. Rex said that he had gone to the bar the first night in town looking for a place to stay, and that someone had gotten him drunk and stolen his poke. The gal had apparently rescued him, taken him in, and a romance had developed. All they had brought with them was a half-gallon of vodka and a new pair of rubber boots.

I figured he had gotten himself drunk and spent the money, but I bit my tongue and didn't say anything. The rest of the gang wandered off one by one to suffer their disappointment in private. My jaws were pretty tight too, so I got up and went out the back door to cool off, leaving Rex and his sweetie alone in the living room.

I was on the back porch, splitting kindling and grumbling to myself, when I heard Rex cut loose with a string of cuss words that would have scorched the paint off a battle ship. I went in to see what was happening. He was sitting in his chair with one of his brand new boots in his lap. He had decided to cut the top off his old ones to make slippers out of them, and had picked up one of the new ones by mistake. To top it off, he had cut the top off the right one, which was the one that leaked in his old pair. I figured it served him right, considering the fact he had blown our money on likker. I went back to the woodpile and left him muttering in his chair. Sometimes there is justice in the world, after all.

One day Rex decided he was going to make a hunting knife out of an old butcher knife he had found in the shed. It was too long and thick for his taste, so he was attempting to file it down to size. He worked on it many days, and was making little progress with the worn-out files that we had.

In the shed was an old, sandstone-grinding wheel. The stone was about two feet in diameter, the kind that is usually mounted on a bicycle-like frame; you pumped pedals to make it spin slowly.

There was also a 4 horsepower Briggs & Stratton engine in the shed that powered a small gold dredge. Rex got the bright idea that he could spin the grindstone with the motor and finish his knife in a hurry. He was busy for days in the shop, banging around and acting mysterious. I knew what he was up to but decided to stay out of it.

One day I heard the little Briggs fire up and grunt as it took the load. In a moment, I could hear the sound of the stone on metal. The motor gradually built up RPM. Suddenly, there was a loud bang and the motor revved up to full speed. Rex stumbled out of the shed, rubbing his eyes and cussing up a blue streak.

That old, soft, sandstone-grinding wheel was only meant to turn at a few RPM, and the little Briggs had gradually built up the speed until the stone couldn't handle the centrifugal force. It had exploded, throwing pieces of rock in all directions.

It was a miracle Rex wasn't hurt. The big pieces had missed him and he was only spattered with pebbles. It was enough to tear his coat and break the skin in several places on his hands and face. One chunk of rock flew up and knocked a hole in the shingles on the roof. The knife blade flew across the room and buried its pointy end in the wall. The accident kind of put the knife project on hold for a while, but he did eventually finish it. It turned out okay and he used it as long as I knew him.

He had one other invention that caused quite a stir in the saloons of Ketchikan when he made his annual trip to town. Rex had done some marten trapping the winter before, and he had several nice pelts that he had tanned. He worked for weeks on a hat made out of two of them that looked like Davy Crocket's 'coonskin hat.

It was made of one big pelt wrapped around the sides, and another flattened out on top with the head hanging down in front. He had dried the skull, then put it inside the head skin and installed two big, red glass beads for eyes. He rigged a rubber band to hold the jaw closed and ran a string back through the hat to hang down behind his ear. He could reach up and pull the string, and the jaw would open and close.

It was an evil looking thing. With the hat on and his huge gray beard, he looked like something out of a Frederick Remington painting. He could cage drinks in the bars for days with that hat, and one tourist offered him five hundred bucks for it. He took the drinks but kept the hat.

March came in like a lion; it warmed up into the forties and rained. This was worse than the snow and cold. There was nothing to do but sit around the house and read. We were all kind of sick of each other's company and it was pointless to try to do anything outside.

One morning we sat drinking coffee and looking out the living room window at the dismal wet world outside.

"Ya know, if we chop through the ice from the beach on this side to the beach on the other side, all the ice in the bay will float out on the next high tide," Dave said. We allowed that he was probably right, but it would take a heck of a lot of chopping, and the ice looked pretty rotten for walking around on.

"I'm going to try it," he said, tossing down the last of his coffee and heading out the door. We shook our heads and poured another cup. We could hear him hacking away out there all morning. Along in the middle of the afternoon, Rex and I were in the kitchen, I was kneading a batch of bread, and Rex was putting together a pot of beans for dinner. The ring of the ax on the ice had become part of the background noise, and we hadn't been paying much attention to how Dave's project was coming along.

Suddenly we heard him shout. "EEEEEEEEEEEEEETAHHH HHHHHHHH," at the top of his lungs. We looked out the kitchen window and saw him standing on the ice, prying at a widening crack with the ax. He had done it! He had a crack open for a hundred yards across the bay. The tide was going out, and as we watched, the crack gradually widened and the giant iceberg began to drift away. Dave ran back to the beach on our side, bounding from one floating ice cake to the next, until he was on the beach. When he got ashore, he came bursting in the door shouting; "Look at that sucker go, ha ha ha! I told you I could do it."

We congratulated him and thanked him for his efforts. Meanwhile, the tide took all the ice out of the whole bay in one big piece. It looked pretty good to see the bay clear after five months of being locked in behind the ice. We told him he should have carved it into the shape of Texas, but he figured it would be too much work.

SALT CHUCK

Time passed and spring rolled around again. I got an opportunity to work for a mining company as a driller's helper that summer. I worked at Rich Hill Mine, which is a couple miles south of Kasaan Village. It wasn't far from home, but I didn't get back to Coal Bay until late August.

During the summer I had become aquainted with a family who had just moved to Happy Harbor, a tiny community on the south end of Kasaan Island. We used the beach in front of their property as a staging area for getting people and equipment up to the mine. We could fly supplies and people to Happy Harbor by float plane from Ketchikan, then helicopter it up to the mine on Kasaan Mountain.

Bob Bennett and his family were building a big A-frame house. They were living in an old boat shed that stood on the beach in front of their property. If we had time to kill, while we were slinging gear up to the camp, they would invite us into their temporary home for coffee.

In August, when we were moving the drill rig off the mountain, we had a lot of food and other miscellaneous items left. The boss was trying to figure what to do with it, so I suggested we drop it off at Bennett's place. He thought that was a great idea, so as we broke the camp down, we threw everything we had no further use for in a cargo net. After the last load from the mine site was loaded on the barge, the chopper dropped the net load of stuff and me on the beach in front of Bennett's place.

They were glad to get the food and various other things we had piled in the net, and invited me into their home to wait for the floatplane to Ketchikan. They poured me a cup of coffee and we traded yarns until the plane came for me. I told them I lived nearby and they invited me to stop by whenever I was in the neighborhood. It was the beginning of a good friendship, and many of the adventures I was to have in the next few years would be with these people.

I went on into town and spent most of my savings on a 4-horse outboard and a brand new Remington rifle. The gun was a 7MM magnum with a 3-9 variable scope. It turned out to be a pretty useless rifle for the country where I lived. The barrel was too long, the scope was awkward and hard to keep dry, and the bullets were too explosive at short-range. Most of the deer and the one bear I had killed in the past two years were shot at fifty yards or less. I discovered that those hi-velocity bullets ruined a lot of meat. That rifle was better suited for plains hunting than the dense forests of Southeast Alaska. I eventually traded it for a 7.62 Argentine Mauser with a peep sight. The gun came with a complete set of reloading tools and enough components to last forever.

When the money was spent, I went home to Coal Bay and settled in for the third winter. As the fall progressed, I found myself less than excited about spending another winter cooped up in that old house with the same people.

During the summer at Rich Hill, I had become acquainted with a logger named Dave Sallee, who also lived at Happy Harbor. He had cut some trees that were in the way of our operation, and while he was living in the camp with us, Dave and I had become good friends. He invited me to come hang out at his place whenever I wanted and hinted that I could work for him part-time, logging on Kasaan Island. At the time, I had a pocketful of money and wasn't very interested in work, but said I would come down and visit if I got a chance.

I had horse-traded Ron Arnce out of a fourteen-foot plywood lifeboat that spring, so one day I loaded some gear in the skiff and rowed down to Happy Harbor. It was a pleasant trip; the water was calm and the little boat rowed well.

I visited around for a few days, and Dave offered me the use of a tiny float house that was attached to his floating camp. I decided to move down for the winter. Dave ran me up to Coal Bay in his skiff to collect the rest of my belongings, and I was soon settled into the tiny float house. It wasn't much, but it had a good barrel stove and it was all mine.

I spent a lot of time with the Bennett family that winter. They had finally moved into their new house and it became the center of activity over the next few months. Bob's wife, Iva Lee, sort of adopted me into the family and there was a place set for me at the dinner table every night. If I didn't show up, she would send one of the boys to find me.

They were a great bunch to hang out with, and we had a lot of fun trapping mink, hunting deer, and just kind of getting into anything that came to mind that had entertainment value.

One day somebody made a slingshot and the idea caught on instantly. For the next few days, all the men and boys were whittling alder crotches and lashing on any kind of rubber we could scrounge. There was a long, crescent beach behind the house that was covered with pea gravel, which made perfect slingshot ammo, and everyone always had a pocketful of small round stones.

Another evening one of the kids made a paper airplane. He was having trouble getting it to fly right, and before long everybody in the house was folding paper, trying to make the perfect glider. Over the next few days we progressed to elaborate planes made out of cardboard and Styrofoam egg cartons. Some of them even sported hand carved propellers and rubber band motors. We eventually got bored and used them for shotgun practice.

We were short of small skiffs that you could put an outboard motor on, so we started experimenting with motorized rafts. I built the first one out of four small cedar logs. It had a wooden box for a seat, and my little 4-horse hanging on the back. It worked after a fashion but looked rather strange running around in the harbor. It rode so low in the water that the raft was nearly invisible. All you could see was me sitting on a box and the outboard behind me.

One evening I decided to try to jig up a couple bottom fish for dinner. It was flat calm out in the bay, so I figured I dared go out of the harbor on my raft. There is a twenty-fathom ledge just outside the harbor entrance that is alive with bottom fish, so I motored out to the edge and dropped a hook over, baited with a clam. It hardly hit the bottom before I felt a sharp tug. I yanked the rod tip up to set the hook and the fish immediately took off, stripping line off the reel against the drag.

It was really pulling hard and I had to keep lightening up on the drag to keep it from pulling me over. The tiny raft wasn't exactly what you would call a stable platform, and it was obvious that I had hooked something big. Every time the fish would stop pulling I would reel in a few feet of line.

Gradually the fish tired out and I was able to reel it to the surface. It was a big halibut, and when it finally came up behind the raft it looked as long as my crude boat. The fish took one look at me and went straight toward the bottom. Eventually I coaxed it back to the surface.

It was obvious that the fish was too big to bring aboard, and I had no way to kill it. The only thing I could think of to do was try to tow it back to the dock and find some help. I eased the fish around behind the raft and while holding the pole tip high, I set the throttle on the motor and yanked the starting rope. The little Evenrude caught on the first pull and roared to life. The raft moved, and before the halibut could respond I pulled his head out of the water and opened the throttle wide open.

It was quite a balancing act. I had to steer the raft, while keeping enough tension on the rod to keep the fish's head above the surface. I knew that if I let it get a purchase on the water all would be lost. I made it through the narrow, shallow harbor entrance and made the turn toward Bob Bennett's dock. As I passed the float I yelled for help, but no one heard me.

The next house up the beach was "Boots" McAllister's place. As I towed the fish past her dock, I could see Boots and her partner, Tom, sitting at the kitchen table. I waved frantically and pointed into the water behind the raft. They waved back, and motioned me to join them for coffee. I made a big circle and came back past the house again, waving for them to come down to the dock. On my third pass, I saw them running down the ramp at top speed. Boots had a pike-pole and Tom was carrying a rifle.

As I passed the dock, I handed the fishing pole to Boots and motored out of the way. The fish went nuts, but Boots knew how to handle it. She soon had it alongside the float, and Tom put a couple .22 bullets through its head. By the time I got the raft tied up, they had pulled the fish out on the dock with the pike-pole and were standing there admiring it. The halibut was a dandy. It weighed about 75 pounds and fed everyone in the harbor for several days.

The next raft I built was made of two timbers split out of a cedar log, fastened together with crosspieces notched into the main beams. Floatation was a big slab of plastic foam that I had beachcomed, and the deck was a scrap of 3/4-inch plywood nailed to the crosspieces. It worked a little better than the log raft, but not much. There was a lot of drag from the rough surface of the foam, but at least the deck was above the water.

One day I was beachcoambing on the south end of the island, and found two sheets of 1/4-inch plywood. This was a real treasure, and I soon decided to use them to make a better raft. This one was a rectangular scow, about ten inches thick and slanted up in front. I used two two-by-tens for the sides, and the two sheets of plywood for the deck and bottom. It had a frame of two-by-twos notched into the side timbers, and a solid transom made out of a two-by-twelve.

I packed the inside with foam egg cartons, plastic bottles with the lids screwed on tight, and any other scraps of floatation material I could find. The project was soon finished with a camo green, black, and brown paint job. We had a launching party one morning after the paint dried, toasting her with Tang when she was finally afloat. The raft worked great and the little Evenrude had just enough power to make it plane if the water was calm. I was quite pleased with her.

Everyone liked the scow so much that a couple more were soon under construction. Bob didn't have an outboard motor small enough, so he mounted a Briggs & Stratton air-cooled engine on deck. The power was transmitted via a propeller shaft with a universal joint at the motor. It worked fine, but was noisy. Elden built a ten-footer with a fifteen-horse outboard and it would really go.

One calm night we got the not-so-bright idea that we could take a car battery and a spotlight and go jacklight a deer. It was highly illegal and not very sporting, but we were a long way out of town and were more interested in fresh meat than sport.

We got everything ready in the afternoon, and after supper we bundled up in our warmest clothes and headed out of the harbor. Elden's raft had more power, so he took the battery and light. His brother, Steve, rode along to run the spotlight while Elden did the driving and shooting. I had a big flashlight taped on my rifle, with a remote switch taped on back by the trigger guard.

It was a pitch-black night and the bay was glassy-flat calm when we left the harbor. We motored around the south end of Kasaan Island and crossed a narrow channel to Daisy Island. We worked our way slowly along in and out of the small bays and inlets, but never did see a deer. We came out of a small inlet called Lenny Bay about eight o'clock, and I noticed that a light breeze had come up out of the south.

Our plan was to cross back over to the West Side of Kasaan Island, then work our way back around the north end to the harbor. As we crossed over, we could feel that the wind had picked up to about fifteen knots. There was a small swell starting to come in off Clarence Strait and the air had warmed considerably.

It dawned on me that a front was moving in and that we better head for home. The harbor entrance was about a mile and a half from the north end of the island. It would be a long hard buck against the southerly swells. If we let them get too big we would not be able to get to the entrance.

I cruised alongside Elden's raft and signaled him to slow down so we could talk. I pointed out the clouds moving in overhead and the warm breeze coming in off the strait, and we decided to cut for home around the south end. As we approached the south end of the island, the wind was increasing and the swells had grown to about three feet. Waves were starting to break over the bows of the rafts, and we soon had to slow down to keep from getting wet.

Just as we made the turn around the end of the island, my engine quit. Elden was behind me, so he came alongside and took me in tow while I tinkered on the engine. I figured it was water in the gas, so I switched to a spare tank and flushed out the filter on the pump. I drained the carburetor float bowl, then squeezed the primer bulb until it came up hard. It took about ten cranks to work the water out of the combustion chambers, but it finally sputtered to reluctant life.

Elden cast off the towline and we kept going. The wind was up to about twenty knots by then and the swells were about five feet. It was pretty scary perched on top of those boxes, rolling up and over the big waves. The only reason we were able to keep going was that the crests were about fifty feet apart so the boats could recover from one before we had to deal with the next one.

When we turned east, to cross the end of the island, it really got difficult. We were running parallel to the seas, and it felt like I was going to fall off as the raft rolled up and over the steep waves. We were barely making any headway and it seemed to take forever to get around the end of the island.

Eventually, we began to bend around to the north and take the waves more on the stern. This eased the motion somewhat, and I realized that we were probably out of danger. It actually started to be fun to feel a big wave come up from behind and push the raft along the surface like a surfboard.

We were making better time, and before long we turned west into the harbor entrance. It was a relief to get into the calm water, but it was kind of a letdown too. The night had turned into an adventure and I realized it was over. We were pretty glad to go into the cheery warmth of the house, and we had a tale to tell.

During the winter, Bob decided he wanted to build a new wing on the north side of the house. There was an old float house in the salt chuck at the head of Kasaan Bay. A logging company had left it behind, and Bob made a deal with the owner to tear it down for the lumber.

We all moved to the chuck in the spring and I made my own camp across the bay. I helped with the work part of the time, and did a lot of exploring around the area when I wasn't working with them. Salt Chuck was an interesting place. There were several old mines to poke around in, and since nobody had lived there for many years there was a lot of wildlife. We got there in early May and started seeing bears every day.

One morning we were standing around the campfire drinking coffee and planning the day's work. Bob's wife came out of the tiny shack they were camping in and said, "Hey, there's a bear on the beach at the south end of the bay; why don't you guys go shoot it? Some fresh meat would taste good and I want to can some up for next winter."

We thought that was a great idea, so Bob and his nephew, Dave McGillvray, decided they would do the honors. It was a pretty good setup for a stalk, so they grabbed their rifles and took off in the rowboat. They rowed quietly along the west shore until they were about a quarter mile down wind of the bear. There was a small cove where they could anchor the skiff out of sight of the bear.

They landed as quietly as they could, then started sneaking along the beach toward where the critter was feeding. We could see the whole drama unfolding perfectly from where we were standing; the bear feeding contentedly in the grass on the point, and Bob and Dave working their way slowly along the beach....

As the bear fed, he walked behind a big cedar log that had been lying on the beach for several years. It was about four feet in diameter, forty feet long, and the bear was completely hidden behind the log. There was a strip of grass between the log and the trees, and we could see that he hadn't gone into the woods.

When the hunters rounded the last point to the section of beach where they knew the bear was feeding they couldn't see him. They continued to walk quietly along the beach until they were standing in front of the log that the bear was hidden behind. They stopped and looked around, then took out cigarettes and lit up. They were standing with their backs to the log, smoking their cigarettes and talking, when the bear stood up on its hind legs right behind them. We were going nuts, jumping up and down, waving our arms and shouting. Suddenly the guys turned around and did the wildest double take I have ever seen. They both took off for the water and never even tried to shoot. Meanwhile the bear said "woof," then vanished into the timber.

Bob and Dave were pretty embarrassed. We all had a good laugh, and the story has been told many times since. The bears probably still tell it too.

LINDEMAN CREEK

A few days later, I was outside the Salt Chuck exploring around among the small islands in the northwest end of Kasaan Bay. It was one of those special spring evenings, warm and windless with a high overcast. The tide was in, and I was idling along the shore just south of Lindeman Creek. As I passed the mouth of the bay, I saw a bear feeding in the sedge grass on the north bank of the creek. I knew Bob and his family still wanted to can some meat, so I decided to try to shoot the bear.

I anchored the raft on the south point, loaded my rifle and slipped into the timber. There was a good game trail just inside the woods that made for easy going, and in a few minutes I was in the edge of the trees across the creek from the bear. There was an old cedar snag that had blown down onto the beach many years ago. I slipped along behind it out onto the beach, keeping the log between the bear and myself. The log lay at a slight angle to the shore and was almost perpendicular to the line of sight between the bear and myself. I figured it would make a good rest.

I got into position about halfway down the log. I could kneel behind it and anchor the gun down real steady. There was a faint breeze coming down the creek from right to left, and the bear was completely unaware of my presence. I wiggled around till I was comfortable, then took a sight picture on him.

I was about sixty yards from the bear. He was facing away from me, quartering slightly to the left. When his head was down it was partly hidden by the left shoulder. When he raised it to look around, between bites of sedge grass, the head was moving too much for a shot. I moved the front bead to the body behind the left shoulder. It looked like I had a good lineup through the chest cavity to the off shoulder. I figured I could drive the bullet through the chest and break that leg as it exited.

This was pretty optimistic, considering the gun I was using. The little 7.62 cartridge is not as powerful as a .308, and I had loaded it down a bit because the rifle was almost fifty years old. Also, the magazine spring had broken during the winter, so it was essentially a single shot. I had a rag stuffed in the magazine well with an extra shell on top of it under the bolt. To reload, I had to eject the spent case, then lower the muzzle and shake the second cartridge into the chamber. It worked but wasn't very fast. Definitely not what you could call a bear gun! I was about to get a lesson in the fundamentals of bear shooting that would make a lasting impression on me.

I drew in a breath, let some out, and when the sights looked right, I squeezed off the shot. BOOOM......WHAKK. As the rifle recoiled, I saw the bear go down. I stood up to reload, and as I did, the bear got up, spun around, and came straight at me. I stood there gawking for about one heartbeat, then ran to the left into the water. The bear jumped over the log right at the place I had shot from and vanished into the woods.

So there is the mighty white hunter, standing up to his behind in the water with an empty rifle in his hands and a stupid look on his face. When my brain finally started functioning again, I shoved the other round in the chamber and waded ashore. I squelched over to the log and peered into the woods.

It was almost dark, and the last thing I wanted to do was go in there alone looking for a wounded bear. I sat down on the log and emptied the water out of my boots. When I was finished, I went into the edge of the timber hoping he was lying there dead. I knew without a doubt that I had put the bullet right into his chest, so he probably wouldn't go far.

There was one skid mark just inside the trees and nothing else. I made a short careful circle, hoping to find a blood trail, but it was getting too dark to see much of anything in the woods. I decided to go home and come back with help in the morning.

Dave, Elden and I went back at first light to look for the bear. Dave had a black mutt, named Shadow, who loved to chase bears. We took him along, hoping the dog could sniff out the carcass.

When we arrived at Lindeman Creek, we went to where the bear had been standing when I shot him. We were hoping to get some indication as to how badly he was hurt. I was pretty familiar with the old Mauser, and positive I had hit him where I was aiming. We found a few black hairs, but nothing else.

We moved to where the bear had disappeared into the woods and looked the area over carefully. Dave let the dog off the leash and told him to find the bear. Shadow took off up the hill and didn't come back for several hours. I don't think he ever found the bear; he always barked at them and we would have heard the commotion.

While the dog was gone, we searched the whole peninsula on the south side of the creek, but never found any trace of the bear. I suspect I missed the heart. The bullet probably went through the lungs and stopped in the flesh under the right shoulder, but didn't have enough energy to break the bone. I don't think the bullet exited the body, because an expanded bullet makes a large hole coming out and there is usually some blood. The blood must have coagulated in the hair around the tiny entrance wound, and none ever fell to the ground.

I learned five lessons with that bear. Use a rifle and bullet combination that will shoot through the body from any angle. Never hunt alone. Shoot early enough in the day so as to have time to follow up if the animal is wounded. Never shoot a potentially dangerous animal in the body if you have a choice. The only shot that will get an instant kill is either through the brain or by breaking the neck forward of the front shoulders. I have been involved in the shooting of many bears over the years and everyone we shot in the body got into the woods. There was only one other that we never found, but even two in a lifetime are too many.

The fifth and probably most important lesson from this incident had to do with my choice of locations from which to fire the shot. The log I was hiding behind was at the closest point of timber to the bear. What I interpreted as a charge, was just the bear running to the closest shelter available.

It was mostly lack of experience that caused us to lose those bears. There was nobody to teach us how to do it right, and we didn't have access to the books by experienced hunters that I was fortunate enough to read in later years. A wounded bear in heavy cover is an adventure I can do without.

Lindeman Creek seemed to have some special draw on me and over the years I spent quite a lot of time there. One summer I camped for a few weeks under the branches of a big spruce tree that stood on the beach at the head of the bay.

There were the remains of an old homestead on the north side of the bay. It had been so long-abandoned that there was nothing left of the old buildings but several piles of rotten boards. I never was able to find out much information about the people that lived there. Their name was Lindeman, and they grew vegetables in a large garden that they sold to the mine over at Salt Chuck. They probably starved out when the mine closed after W.W.I.

The main thing they had left behind was a large clearing at the head of the bay where their gardens had been. The big spruce that sheltered my camp that summer stood in the center of the lower edge of the clearing. Its lower branches hung all the way to the ground on the gravel beach in front of the meadow. I had broken off some of the dead lower limbs of the tree, opening up a small, natural shelter that shed all but the heaviest rain. I built a bunk out of boards that I scrounged from one of the old buildings, and suspended a tarp over it to keep off the few raindrops that found their way down through the branches.

The room under the limbs was large enough to allow me to keep a small fire inside. I made a backrest so I could sit by the fire and read by the light it provided. All in all, it was one of the most comfortable camps that I have ever enjoyed.

One evening, I was sitting by the fire, reading James Michener's book, Hawaii. It was a cool, humid, spring night, the warmth of the fire was very pleasant. About eleven o'clock, after the spring sun had finally sunk behind the mountains to the northwest, I saw a flicker of movement out of the corner of my eye. I looked toward the fire where I had seen the motion and saw a large toad sitting, gazing intently into the flames. As I watched him, another toad hopped into the circle of light and joined the first one. They were about a foot out from the ring of rocks that I used to contain the fire, and seemed utterly fascinated as they looked into the glowing embers.

Suddenly more toads appeared, and at the end of an hour there were seven of them lined up around the fire, warming themselves and staring fixedly into the flames. They looked like worshipers gathered around some ancient god. I suppose to a creature that has no body heat other than what he can absorb from his surroundings, that fire was god-like to them. They could probably sense the heat from many yards away and the light and warmth that it offered was irresistible.

More of them gathered around the fire as I watched in wonder. Eventually I felt the bunk calling and moved carefully through the worshipers to my bed. They seemed unaware of my presence, and as I lay in my blankets, drifting off to sleep in the flickering firelight, I felt a strange kinship with these simple dwellers of the forest. Their ancestors probably still tell the legend of the night the sun god appeared under the big spruce at the edge of the meadow.

In the morning they were gone. I watched for them every night, but they never came again. They surely must have been able to see the light from my fire at night, but why they never came again is a mystery to me.

After I had camped there for several weeks, my food supply was getting pretty low. I still had plenty of staples, but I was out of jam and raisins and other sweets. I did have sugar, but was living on bread and beans most of the time. One sunny morning in late June I was poking around up in the meadow behind camp. The Thimbleberry patch was well leafed-out and there were hundreds of white blossoms scattered among the foliage. I was standing in the morning sun, enjoying the view, when I noticed a patch of darker green farther back among the leaves. I pushed my way in among the tall bushes, and lo and behold, I found a clump of rhubarb stalks that reached all the way up to the top of the Thimbleberry plants! The rhubarb leaves were lying on top of the berry leaves seven feet off the ground. Some of the stalks were two inches in diameter! What a treasure!

I took out my sheath knife and whacked out a section of one about two feet long. I hurried back to camp, stirred up the embers of my morning fire and added more driftwood. When the fire was crackling, I mixed up a batch of pie dough in a bowl. When it was ready, I pinched off several chunks the size of golf balls and rolled them out flat on a board. I cut the rhubarb into small piles in the center of each circle of dough, then added a couple tablespoons of sugar. I folded each one in half and wet the edges to stick them together in order to seal in the rhubarb and sugar.

When I had several ready, I raked some coals out of the fire and put my big cast-iron skillet on them to heat. When water would sizzle in the oil, I put in two of the pastries and carefully browned them on both sides. When they were done, I laid them on the board and sprinkled more sugar on each one. While the first two cooled I fried up the next two, and they got the same treatment when they were finished.

I could hardly contain myself. I bit into the first pie and was immediately in heaven. You have to live for a time without some food you normally take for granted to really appreciate it. Just that simple addition to my diet changed my attitude enough that a camping trip that I was considering ending the day before turned into several more weeks of pleasant exploration of the area. You must suffer lack to really appreciate the basic, simple pleasures of life.

I really enjoyed Lindeman Creek, so one fall I built a tiny cabin in the timber just west of the meadow. It was seven hatchet-handles wide and ten long. It had a dirt floor and the roof was made of poles covered with plastic and moss. I made a door out of beachcomed lumber and a stove out of a thirty-gallon grease barrel that I scrounged at Salt Chuck mine. It was warm and cozy and I spent time there quite often.

One winter morning I awakened to find fresh snow on the ground. I was out of meat, so I decided to take advantage of the good tracking the new snow would provide. There was an old logging road in the edge of the timber near the head of the creek. I decided to follow it up the valley to the old logging works on the mountain above the bay. I hunted my way slowly up the valley, and after about half-an-hour I came to the edge of the first clear-cut. There was a low hill on the right side of the old road. I decided to climb up on top of it so I could sit in the morning sun and look out over the logged-off area.

I struggled up the brushy slope to the top of the ridge, then climbed up on a big stump. From my perch I could look out over another small valley. About a hundred yards from my stump stood a Bull Moose! At first I didn't know what it was. It was obviously a large, brown animal with a hump in its back and at first I thought it was a bear. In a moment it raised its head and I realized what it was.

There are no moose on Prince of Wales Island, or at least I had heard that there were none. But there I was looking at one. It was in easy rifle range and my first inclination was to shoot it. It only took me a moment to reject the idea, though. I thought it would be a shame to shoot it because, if left alone, it might produce more moose, and it would sure be nice to have an abundance of them this close to home. Also, I was alone and a mile off the beach. It would have taken days to pack out the meat and I had no way to store it.

I watched the young bull feed in the creek bottom for a while until he moseyed on down the valley and disappeared into the timber. I saw sign of it several more times over the next couple winters. Eventually I heard that the Fish and Game Department had planted a pair of them in the Thorne Bay area a few years earlier. I have no idea what happened to them, but by the late-70s they seemed to have disappeared from the area. I suspect that either the wolves got them, or some yahoo shot one or both. Too bad; it would sure be nice to be able to hunt moose on Prince of Wales Island.

One sunny, winter afternoon I was sitting on the beach near my cabin. The sun was warm and my chores were done for the day. I was whittling on a stick and day dreaming about one thing or another when I heard a shrill scream up the beach to the west. At the sound, my head turned and my eyes automatically searched for the source of the racket. About a hundred yards up the beach I saw two marten running towards me. There was a small, raggedy-looking one being chased by a larger animal. After a few yards the little one would stop, and they would roll around on the beach screaming, growling, and hissing like a couple of mad tomcats. After a brief fight, the little one would break free and take off towards the head of the bay.

They passed about ten feet from where I was sitting, then fought their way down to the creek. They crossed the creek, then fought their way up the beach across the cove from me. They soon rounded the south point and disappeared. I could hear their screams fade into the distance as they fought their way around the next bay. The whole scene took only about two minutes from start to finish and left me grinning to myself with the humor of it. I suspect it might have been mating season and they were having a dispute over territory. I never saw them again, so I don't know who won.

Another afternoon, a big black and tan male wolf trotted past and eventually disappeared around the south point. He also passed within a few feet of me without sensing my presence. It has always amazed me how, if you spend enough time in a place, you gradually become part of the scene. The natural inhabitants of the place go on with their business as if you weren't there.

I never made any attempt to hide or be quiet. After a few days the place would gradually come alive with birds, squirrels, deer, and the other members of the animal community. One pair of local residents that always got a chuckle out of me was a pair of mallard ducks that spent each night in the grass at the mouth of the creek. About dark each night they would fly in from the west and the hen would land in the mouth of the creek. The drake would fly on up the valley, quacking like crazy. After circling the area, he would stop quacking and everything would get real quiet for a few minutes. Then all of a sudden he would come swooping down the creek at about mach 3 and buzz the old lady. This would set off a cacophony of quacking by both of them as the male circled the bay, then came back and landed in the mouth of the creek.

When the nightly ritual was finished, they would climb out on the bank and spend the night hidden in the tall sedge grass along the creek. I think the male flew up the valley to check for predators, but the buzzing routine was obviously done purely for the fun of it.

The remains of my little cabin are about gone now, and the mountain behind it has all been logged. The land has changed, but it still remains unchanged in my memories.

MAD SOW

A week after losing the bear at Lindeman Creek, I had another encounter to aid me in my education process. I was visiting at the float-house project one morning. On the way back to my camp, I decided to take a tour of the north end of the bay.

There is an island in the middle of Salt Chuck Bay that divides the big lagoon into two parts. The island is about a mile long and a quarter-mile wide. On the north end is an old clear-cut that was logged back in the late fifties.

When the loggers cut the patch, for some reason they left a bunch of tall, skinny spruce trees standing on the point. Over the years, some of these trees along the north edge of the clear-cut have blown down in the winter gales that roar across these parts. The blown-down timber is like a bunch of jackstraws piled at random with a few trees still standing among them. There is a tiny patch of undisturbed trees on the very tip of the point.

As I idled the skiff along the West Side of the island, I saw a bear on the beach at the north end of the clear-cut. The bear heard my outboard about the same time I saw it, and it vanished into the brush among the blowdowns. I thought I might be able to see it again in the clear-cut.

I beached the skiff, loaded the old Mauser, and pushed up the brushy trail through the blowdowns to the edge of the cut. At the last of the blowdown, I climbed up on a log that was lying parallel with the edge of the slash. There was a tall, slender, spruce tree a few feet to my left that had somehow survived the winter winds, and to my front was the clearing. It was a hell-tangle of berry bushes, devil's club, and rotting limbs.

As I stood there looking out over the opening, the bear rose up on its hind legs about ten feet in front of me. There was a clump of berry bushes between us, and all I could see was its head silhouetted in the morning sun. Without thinking, I threw the rifle to my shoulder and fired.

When I recovered from the recoil, the bear was gone and there was a terrible screaming noise coming from overhead. I looked toward the noise and what I saw raised the hair on the back of my neck. About fifty feet off the ground, among the first branches of the tree to my left, was a tiny cub! He was looking down at me, yelling at the top of his lungs.

I looked back toward the bush where the other bear had been a few seconds ago and saw the bear moving quickly off to my right. It suddenly dawned on me that I was in trouble! The bear I had shot at was obviously the mother of the cub in the tree, and she was circling around to defend her offspring.

I ejected the empty cartridge case from the chamber of the old Mauser, and shook the spare in to replace it. As I closed the bolt, I ran up the log past the tree where the cub was screaming. I climbed up on another tree trunk that lay across the log, about ten feet from where I had been standing when I fired the shot at the sow. There was another standing tree beside this log similar to the one the cub was in.

I got behind the trunk and leaned my left shoulder against it to steady the rifle, then aimed the gun toward the base of the other tree. Within seconds the sow appeared on the other log. One moment there was nothing there, and the next she appeared right where I had been standing when I had shot at her.

Her head moved quickly from side to side, and as she turned toward me, she looked me square in the eye. She was quartering toward me about fifteen feet away, and I could see her gather herself up to leap at me. I moved the front bead to her neck and pulled the trigger. The rifle fired, and the last thing I saw as the gun recoiled was the bear falling limply off the log.

When I recovered from the recoil she had vanished. The cub was still screaming overhead, so I cleared the chamber of the rifle and pulled two rounds from the loops on my belt. I dropped one into the breech and the other onto the rag in the magazine well, then closed the bolt. I pointed the rifle back at the place she had been and stood there waiting to see if she would reappear.

There was no movement in the bushes, and after a few moments I walked slowly down my log and stepped onto the other one. I could see a patch of fur in a hole off the left side of the log. I approached, and the bear's head came into view. She looked very dead. I could see the exit wound in the back of the neck, and it was obvious that the bullet had passed through the neck and broken the spine as it exited.

I climbed into the hole and tried to wrestle the carcass up onto the log, but it was hopeless. She probably weighed 250 pounds and I was going to need some help. I climbed out of the hole and looked up at the pathetic little cub in the tree. He was clinging to the trunk, looking down at me, and every so often he would let out a terrible scream.

I scrambled back out to the beach and went back to the floathouse where my friends were working. The men all piled in the skiff and we motored back to the end of the island. When we arrived at the scene, the cub had vanished. We wrestled the sow out of the hole and down to the skiff, then went back to look for the cub. We never did find it and I have no idea if it survived. It was early in the spring, and it had been nursing, so it probably was too young to fend for itself. It still saddens me to think of that little guy starving to death over the next few weeks. If I had known the bear had a cub, I would never have shot at her the first time.

We feasted on fresh bear meat and Iva Lee canned up the rest for leaner times. I occupied myself for the next few days fleshing the hide and salting it down to preserve it until I could set up a tanning vat.

The spring passed without further bear hunts and we moved back to Happy Harbor just before the Coho salmon season started in mid-June. I went off to a drilling job and the rest of the gang went fishing for the summer.

When fall came, I had to find another home for the winter. The tiny logging outfit that owned the float house I was living in was breaking up, so my house would go with the rest of the camp when it left. Elden had been slowly building a small log house near the Bennett place and it was finished enough to be habitable. Elden had a girlfriend in the Lower 48. He decided to go down and see if he could talk her into marrying him. He offered me the use of his cabin while he was gone.

The place was warm and comfortable, but we had a terrible plague of mice that winter. The moss chinking in the log walls was an open invitation to them. By November, when things started freezing up, the mouse community had moved in with me. The minute I would blow out the lamps at night the house would come alive with the sound of mice scurrying around, scavenging for anything edible.

Elden had insulated between the roof sheeting and the ceiling with fiberglass insulation. The abominable little critters loved it. They must have had tunnels through the insulation because I could hear them scamper across the ceiling from one end of the cabin to the other. They would ransack the kitchen every night, carrying off everything edible that they could find. They gnawed the plastic lid off my peanut butter can and ruined that and got into my rice, beans, macaroni, butter, etc. They even galloped up and down my body while I was sleeping. One time I woke up in the middle of the night and found one curled up in my hair, asleep. That was it; I declared war.

I found five mousetraps in the shed and just before bedtime I baited them with peanut butter and scattered them around on the kitchen counter. I crawled into bed and blew out the lamp. In moments I could hear the pitter-patter of tiny mouse feet in the ceiling. Then suddenly, SNAP! Scrape, scrape, scrape, scrape. Oh, the satisfaction I reveled in as I listened to the first mouse kick out his death throes. Moments later, WHACKA! Another one bit the dust. YA!

In ten minutes, all five traps were full. I got out of bed to run my trapline. I pitched the corpses out the back door and reset the traps. While I worked, I could feel hundreds of beady eyes staring at me from the walls. I didn't care—this was war! I can't remember how many mice I caught before I finally fell asleep in exhaustion, but by morning I only had two functional traps left.

The next night at lights-out it was as if I had not eliminated a single mouse. If anything, there were more than before. They were springing spontaneously out of the soil and heading straight for my cabin to re-enforce their legions. My two remaining traps wore out in the first couple hours, and I finally fell asleep planning a new campaign for the next night.

I got up at first light, had a quick breakfast, and then went to work on the ultimate mousetrap. I cut the top out of a five-gallon Blazo can and punched holes across from each other just below the rim. Next, I cut a piece of wire out of an old coat hanger and bent a "U" in the middle. I wired a metal rectangle of sheet metal cut from a piece of stovepipe onto the stiff wire and inserted the resulting contraption into the holes in the top of the can.

This device was arranged so that one end of the flap rested on the edge of the can, and the other was suspended in mid-air over the middle of the can. When the trap was finished, I poured about a gallon of water in the bottom and smeared some peanut butter on the suspended end of the flap. It was absolutely ingenious. A self-resetting trap that could hold a hundred dead mice. I gloated all day and could hardly wait until dark.

Just before bedtime, I placed the trap on the kitchen counter against the wall. The end of the flap made a catwalk out to the bait. When the mouse crossed the axle wire, his weight would cause the flap to tip down and dump him into the water. When his weight disappeared the long end of the flap, being heavier, would fall back onto the rim of the can. The trap would be reset and ready for the next victim.

I went to bed early and once again, within moments after the light went out, the mouse-world came to life. I chuckled to myself as I lay listening to them scurrying toward the kitchen. I soon heard mouse claws on metal, then a splash and a clunk as the trap reset itself.

Then I heard the sound of frantic scratching on the wall of the metal can as the mouse tried desperately to climb out of the trap. The sound went on, and on, and on until I was ready to scream. Images of a tiny, pink mouse nose struggling for breath as the feet scratched hopelessly at the slick metal of the walls of the trap filled my mind. Finally his struggles slowed, then faded away. The house was silent for a while, then I heard tiny feet moving again in the kitchen. In moments the trap clanked, and the horrible racket of another mouse in his death-throes filled the house.

By midnight I couldn't stand it anymore. There were five mice in the trap and each one had taken about fifteen minutes to drown. I got up and pitched the contraption out the back door.

I eventually got used to my tiny neighbors rattling around all night. I didn't even mind them running around on the bed as long as they stayed out from under the covers. So a kind of truce prevailed for a few days.

The hardest thing about the dark months of a northern winter is finding enough things to do to keep from getting bored. You can only read so many books. Soon the neighbors have heard all your stories and you have heard theirs. The ability to entertain yourself is what eventually separates the true hivernants from those who can't live away from the diversions that the city life has to offer.

One evening I was sitting in my chair in the dark, just sort of letting my mind roam from one subject to another. Overhead in the ceiling I could hear the sound of skittering feet, and in the kitchen they were trying to gnaw off the cupboard doors. After one unusually loud thump, I flicked on the flashlight and pointed the beam toward the noise. There were several of the nasty little critters on the counter. As I watched them scurry for cover, I seized upon an idea that would alleviate boredom and trim down the mouse population at the same time.

First, I wired a remote switch into my 6-volt flashlight. Next, I put a round of firewood on the kitchen counter and made a ramp up in front of it with a scrap of kindling. One end of the ramp was on the counter and the other on a book in front of the block of wood. Next, I rigged a rifle rest in front of my chair and arranged the flashlight so it shined on the end of the ramp. When it was all finished I could sit comfortably in my chair with the lights out and wait until I heard a mouse gnawing on the bait. Then I could flick on the flashlight and shoot the little blighter before he disappeared. After the bullet passed through the mouse it would lodge safely in the chunk of wood, and other than ruining the mouse's day, no damage would be done. "Ingenious, absolutely ingenious! Heh, heh, heh," I gloated to myself with a maniacal twinkle in my eye.

When everything was set I smeared peanut butter on the upper end of the ramp and retired to my blind. I blew out the kerosene lamp and waited with sweet anticipation for my first victim. It didn't take long. When the light went out, they were in motion. I sat quietly, listening to them scampering through the house.

Pretty soon I heard knawing on the ramp. I snuggled in behind the .22 rifle and hit the toggle switch. Sure enough—there he was! I put the crosshair on him and yanked the trigger. BANG! Dead mouse. "All right." I walked over and tossed the carcass out the back door. I sat back down and turned off the light. It wasn't long before I heard another one at the bait. BANG! Another corpse.

I got about ten that evening before the fun wore off. Each evening, when I tired of my other forms of entertainment, I would set up the shooting gallery and plink a few mice. I wasn't making much of a dent in the mouse population, but I was enjoying my nightly hunts. Before long, Dave and Karl were spending their evenings at my place and we would take turns at the shooting bench.

One night someone cracked a joke about skinning out the little suckers and making pelts out of them. Sounded like a great idea to me, so I made some tiny drying boards and started case skinning them like you would a marten or a mink. Before long, I had a whole string of tiny pelts. Actually, the fur was quite nice, and we speculated at length about the possibility of getting rich selling mouse fur jockstraps in the Lower 48. Alas, this grand scheme, like many others, died of inertia, but I still think we had something there.......

A family named Huckens lived on an old power scow that was beached in a small bight at the north end of the harbor. They had two kids about eight or nine years old and the kids claimed that they had been seeing monsters in the woods at the head of the cove. Their parents wrote it off as kid games and didn't pay much attention to the stories.

One morning I was down at Bob's place for coffee, and when I was ready to leave Bob had followed me out onto the beach. It was a sunny November morning, and we were standing there looking around the harbor, soaking up the warm sun and chatting about one thing or another.

"What the heck is that, a deer?" Bob ask, pointing toward the north end of the bay just to the east of the Huckens place. I looked and could see some kind of animal trotting along the beach.

"Looks like a big wolf to me; maybe that's the monster the Huckens' kids have been seeing," I answered.

"Ought to go shoot the damn thing before it eats one of them," Bob said.

"What's happening?" Dave asked, peering in the direction we were looking. The wolf had gone back into the woods as he came up the stiff-leg from the dock, so there was nothing to see.

"We just saw a wolf down there on the beach. I think you guys should go shoot it before it gets one of the kids. We don't need any of those damn things wandering around on the island," Bob answered.

"I'll go get my rifle. You want to come, Dave?" I asked.

"You bet. I'll pick you up with my skiff at your house," he said, heading back down to his house on the dock. I hurried up the beach to my place and got my rifle and deer call. I knew we would never be able to find the wolf in the woods, but maybe we could call it back out on the beach.

A few moments later Dave picked me up and we motored slowly up to the head of the bay. We pulled the skiff up on a sandy crescent of beach and walked over to a rock pile that would make a good ambush spot. We settled into the rocks, which were about thirty-five yards from the woods, and when we were ready I gave a couple bleats on the fawn call.

The wolf must have been close to the edge of the timber because it appeared instantly. I put the sight bead between the eyes and squeezed off. The wolf went down to the shot and was thrashing around in the sedge grass at the edge of the trees. His death-throes gradually subsided and when he was finally still we got up and walked over to it.

The critter was huge; bigger than the biggest husky you ever saw. He was cream-colored with a black saddle on his back. As we stood there looking at him, his mouth suddenly stretched wide open, then snapped shut with a resounding POP! I whipped the gun to my shoulder and shot him again. We were both quite startled and impressed with the power in those jaws. If your arm had been between them, they would have bitten clear through it.

When we were finally convinced that the beast was dead, we carried it to the boat and headed home. On the way past the Huckens' house, we stopped and asked their kids if this was the monster, and they both agreed that it was. The parents thanked us for disposing of the wolf and said they would take the kids' stories more seriously in the future.

Skinning out that animal was one of the worst chores I ever had the pleasure of enjoying. It was a big male and smelled to highheaven. I worked for parts of three days getting the hide off the carcass, fleshed, and stretched. The thing was eight feet from the tip of his nose to the end of his tail on the stretcher. In the end it was worth the effort though; the hide was beautiful. I wish I still had it, but, alas, I let it go in a horse-trade and never did shoot another one.

Looking back, I'm not sure the wolf was as much a danger to the children as we thought, but who knows. If it had taken one of them, it would have been a terrible tragedy. I figure it was justifiable wolficide.

The rest of the winter was pretty uneventful. The weather was a lot milder and rained a lot. The snowfall that year was minimal and even Coal Bay didn't freeze. Rex spent the winter there by himself that year and I visited with him a few times. We went up and got him for Thanksgiving and he spent a few days with us at the harbor. He had heard from his brother Bob that the niece who owned Coal Bay House was going to donate it to her church, and that he would probably have to move. He was pretty worried about losing his home and seemed depressed.

The long, dark days of winter finally gave way to spring. In April, I followed Bob Bennett and his gang back to Salt Chuck to finish tearing down the float house.

ELDEN'S BEAR

Across from the float house we were tearing down, at Salt Chuck, there was another one room shack we called the Chinaman's cabin. It had been empty since the early fifties but was in good enough condition to be lived in. Elden and his brother Steve had fixed the place up and lived there for a while during trapping season. In the spring, Dave McGillvray and his wife moved in. They spent the summer there while the rest of the gang worked at tearing down the float house across the bay. I camped under the limbs of a big spruce tree, about a hundred yards up the beach from the shack.

Dave and I salvaged some windows out of one of the abandoned buildings at the mine and built a big picture window in the west wall of the cabin. The window displayed a spectacular view of the mountains to the west, and you could also see the south end of the bay.

One sunny May morning I dropped in for coffee. Elden was up from Happy Harbor for a few days and had rowed over for a visit. We were kicked back like Irish lords, sipping boiled coffee out of thick porcelain mugs and yarnin' about one thing or another.

Suddenly Dave pointed out the window and said, "Hey, there's a bear!" We looked where he was pointing, and sure enough, there was a black speck moving along the beach at the south end of the bay.

Elden had never killed a bear and was hoping for a chance during the few days that he was visiting us. We discussed the possibilities for a stalk, and decided that he and I would row across and try to approach the critter upwind along the shore. Dave had some things to do so he decided to stay at the house.

Elden and I took our rifles and headed for the beach. We launched the rowboat as quietly as possible and rowed across to the West Side of the bay. As we rowed we could see the bear feeding along the shore, gradually heading west.

The point of land that he was on was a peninsula that curved around to the south. There was a tidal gut that cut the point off from the mainland and made an island of the peninsula during extreme high tides. The tide was out, so we planned to row past the bear, beach the skiff, and stalk back toward the gut. We hoped to find a good ambush site and shoot across the narrow channel as the bear walked by on the other side; the range would be short. We would have good cover and plenty of time to get into position before the bear arrived.

It was a good plan but didn't quite work out that way. We arrived at our intended ambush point with time to spare. Elden found a good rest over a drift log and everything looked perfect. While we were congratulating ourselves, the bear ambled around the point into view. Elden got ready, but instead of coming our way the bear vanished into the woods with no regard for our carefully laid ambush. We waited a while, hoping he would come back out, but nothing happened. Eventually we gave up and walked across the gut into the timber.

The woods on the hillside in front of us were mostly oldgrowth red cedar and had little underbrush. As we stood there looking around, letting our eyes adjust to the gloom, I saw a flicker of movement straight ahead and above us. About thirty yards away, the bear was clinging to the trunk of a giant red cedar tree. He was about forty feet off the ground with his back toward us. His head was turned our way and he was looking right at us. Elden spotted him about the same time I did. He raised his .270 and fired. The bear fell at the shot and disappeared behind a huckleberry bush at the base of the tree.

"Did you hit him?" I asked.

"I'm not sure. I think he let loose of the tree just as I pulled the trigger," he answered, as he reloaded his rifle.

We waited for a while, then walked over to the tree, rifles ready. There was nothing there. We searched carefully around the base of the tree and a few yards up the hill, but only found a few drops of blood and a small piece of tissue.

We continued to search the whole peninsula in ever-widening circles, but never found another trace of the bear. It was not a very big area and the timber was quite open, but somehow the animal managed to elude us. We went back the next day and looked again, but found nothing. We figured the bullet had just nicked him and that he probably crossed the gut while we searched the hillside. Elden felt pretty bad about injuring the bear, but there was nothing we could do to change it.

Unfortunately, the story doesn't end there. Elden stayed a few more days, then went back to Happy Harbor without seeing another bear. About a week later, Dave and I were coffeeing-up in front of the windows again. As we sat enjoying the view, we saw a bear walking along the beach just west of the peninsula. We were meat-hungry, so we decided to try to shoot it.

The plan was about the same as Elden and I had used a week earlier. The bear was walking toward a small cove just west of the gut where Elden and I had lost the other bear. We would row across the bay to a point downwind of the bear, and shoot across the tiny bay as he walked by. We grabbed our guns, launched the skiff, and rowed across the bay. We anchored the skiff west of the cove and walked quietly up the beach to the point on the West Side of the tiny bay.

There was a pile of boulders on the point that would make a perfect ambush site. We would have good cover and a sixty-yard shot across the cove. We got comfortable among the rocks and I worked out a steady rest, using my coat to cushion the gun. I had a Winchester Model 70 in .270 with a 4 power Weaver scope. Should be a piece of cake. Ha!

About fifteen minutes after we were set, the bear walked slowly around the point and down the beach opposite our hideout. I put the crosshairs on him and followed along, intending to shoot when he was directly across from us. When everything looked right, I squeezed off the shot.

I still didn't have it through my thick head that lung shots weren't always instant killers. Also, I forgot that you have to lead a moving target. The bullet hit too far back and passed through the body just forward of the diaphragm. It clipped both lungs, but didn't damage them enough to be fatal, at least not for a while. The bear didn't even fall down, just hunched up as the bullet passed through him, then turned and vanished into the timber.

We stood up and walked across to the spot where the bear had been when I shot. There were a few hairs and some spots of blood. We went to the edge of the timber and entered carefully with our guns ready. We found blood sign that indicated that it had gone south toward the head of the cove. Things could have not been worse. The trail led into an old clear-cut that had been logged about twenty years before.

Imagine a thick tangle of berry bushes, devil's club, and spruce saplings growing up through a jumble of cedar logs and rotting limbs. The trail was a narrow tunnel about three feet high that had to be negotiated on your hands and knees in most places. The scoped rifle I was carrying would be useless. Luckily, I had a .357 magnum pistol with me and Dave had a sawed-off single-barrel 16-gauge shotgun. We took off our coats and other unnecessary gear, checked the loads in our guns and then crawled into the tunnel.

I worked my way slowly and carefully into the green hell, stopping often to listen and look ahead down the dim path. I found a partial track, then a spot of blood on a leaf. "At least the wound is bleeding,"

I thought to myself, as I crawled along with Dave behind me. Also, I kept flashing back to the image of the bear through the scope. There was something odd about him, but I couldn't quite figure out what it was.

About fifty yards into the tangle, I heard a noise. I looked ahead, and suddenly a black shape scrambled over a big log that blocked the trail about fifteen feet in front of me.

"I just saw him go over that log," I whispered to Dave.

"What do you want to do?" he whispered back. I could see a vein throbbing in Dave's forehead from the tension and excitement of the situation. My heart was pounding too, as adrenaline coursed through my system.

"Let's move up to the log and see if we can see anything from there," I answered.

"Okay," Dave said.

I wiped the sweat off my forehead with my sleeve and crawled on down the trail. When I got to the log, I could see a smear of blood on the moss where the bear had crossed. I peered cautiously over the top but could see nothing. The trail disappeared into a dense thicket of small spruce saplings. The young trees were growing so close together that it looked impenetrable.

As I studied the path ahead, I realized that I could hear a rasping, bubbling sound in the trees ahead. It was the bear breathing! I turned and whispered to Dave, "I can hear him breathing in that patch of dog-hair spruce on the other side of this log." Dave nodded affirmatively and we both looked around, trying to come up with a plan.

The log was perpendicular to the trail. It was about forty feet long and three feet in diameter. The trail crossed it about in the middle, and the left end was buried in a tangle of brush so thick a cat couldn't have gotten through. I was reluctant to go over the log into the spruce trees for fear of spooking the bear deeper into the clear-cut and losing him. I was also worried that he would decide he was cornered and turn to fight us.

I looked off to the right down the length of the log. The brush looked thinner there and the patch of small trees seemed to end about even with the end of the log.

"I'm going to try to work my way around the spruce thicket. When I get in position on the other side, I'll yell for you to come on down the trail. You stay behind the log for a couple minutes after I yell, with your shotgun pointed toward the trail in case he comes back this way. If nothing happens, cross over the log and try to spook him out to me," I said quietly to Dave. He nodded his acceptance of the plan.

As I crawled as quietly as possible along the log, I could still hear the bear breathing. He sounded pretty sick and I hoped he would expire before one of us had to try to shoot him on the run.

When I got to the end of the log, I found that I could stand. I could see the end of another big cedar log that lay parallel to the one we were behind. It was on the other side of the spruce thicket, about fifty feet away. The brush looked thinner there, and I hoped that by climbing up on the other log I would be able to see for a few yards in all directions.

It took about five minutes to push carefully around the end of the thicket and reach the other log. When I got there I crawled up on it, stood up, and looked around. There wasn't much to see, just a sea of berry bushes and more patches of small saplings scattered here and there. I wiped the sweat out of my eyes and brushed a huckleberry leaf off the back sight of the pistol. When I was as ready as I could get, I hollered at Dave, "Okay, Dave! I'm off to your right about forty feet, up on another log. Come on through when you're ready."

"Okay, here I come," he yelled back.

I heard Dave come over the log. At the same instant, I saw movement down at the other end of the log I was standing on. Suddenly the bear lunged up on the end of the log and came straight at me!

Time seemed to slow down to a crawl. A cold spot appeared at the top of my head and spread down my whole body. It was like looking through a tunnel at the bear coming toward me down the log. It seemed like I had all the time in the world. I knew I was going to get just one shot, and it better be perfect. I decided to wait until he was so close I could not miss. I held the pistol out in my right hand, eared back the hammer, and when the bear's head passed under the muzzle, I shot him right between the ears. BANG! The bear rolled off the log, limp as a rag.

Dave pushed his way out of the spruce patch a few feet away and said, "Did you get him?"

I looked at Dave and time started to flow again. I broke into a cold sweat, my gut rolled over, and my knees started shaking. I looked down at the bear then back at Dave and said, "Ya, I got him."

I looked back at the bear. As things gradually came back into focus, I realized that the critter was hardly more than a cub. Dave scrambled over to the bear as I climbed down off the log. We wrestled the carcass up onto the log where we could examine it.

It weighed less than 100 pounds, and as we looked it over we realized it was the same bear that Elden had shot out of the tree a week ago. Elden's .270 bullet had passed through the top of the head, right between the eyes. The bullet had passed through forward of the brain, between the optic nerves, then exited through the lower jaw. Both eyeballs were gone, the tongue was shot away, and the lower jaw bone was hanging by a flap of tissue on the neck.

It was a sickening and gruesome wound, one of the worst I have ever seen. The poor damned critter had been wandering around for a week, totally blind and unable to eat. The pain it had endured must have been horrible. The roots of all the teeth were exposed to the air. If that was not enough, it had taken my .270 bullet through the body and was still able to crawl up on that log and walk under my pistol almost two hours later.

That was the end of our bear hunting for a while. It still sickens me to think of the suffering that animal must have endured. This whole episode illustrates the care and deliberation that must be taken when hunting any animal to ensure that it is killed quickly and cleanly. "Do unto others…"

Dave had yet to kill his first bear. One warm, June morning we were loafing around the Chinaman's shack, trying to figure out a good excuse to avoid anything that involved gainful work. Dave's wife, Pam, was scratching around outside in the garden while we fortified ourselves with caffeine. She came inside and said, "Why don't you lazy bums get off your rumps and go shoot that bear." We looked where she was pointing out the window and saw a black spot moving slowly along the beach at the south end of the bay. Now this was the kind of work we could handle!

"I want to shoot this one; it's my turn," Dave said, finishing his coffee as he got to his feet.

"All right, I'll go get my shootin' iron," I said, setting my cup in the sink and heading out the door. When I got back, Dave had the skiff in the water, and when I was aboard he started rowing across the bay.

The bear was in the southwest corner of the lagoon and the wind was from the west. The tide was high and we would have to try to sneak up on him along the upper edge of the beach. There were many alder trees growing along the edge of the timber and it would not be easy going. We would have to climb over, under, and around hundreds of limbs that overhung the beach.

We beached the skiff a few hundred yards east of the bear and started our stalk. It wasn't easy and I won't bore the reader with all the details. It was a miracle that the bear was still there when we finally crawled up behind an old cedar log about fifty yards from the bear. It was feeding contentedly in the sedge grass just above the water line.

Dave got a steady rest over the log and squeezed off a shot. The bullet hit just behind the left shoulder and I saw it kick up dirt on the bank beyond the bear. When the bullet struck, the bear lunged up the bank, disappearing into the brush behind the alders.

Dave was sure he had passed the bullet through both lungs, so we decided to sit tight for a while and let him bleed out. The hill was clear-cut above the beach and we didn't want to spook it deeper into the brush.

We waited about ten minutes, then Dave went into the edge of the clear-cut behind the alders. I stayed on the beach in case the bear came back out of the brush. We moved slowly and in a few moments we were at the spot where the bear had been standing when Dave fired the shot. Dave was looking for sign in the edge of the woods and I waited to see what he would find. As I stood there, waiting, I realized that I could hear the bear breathing just a few yards from Dave!

"Hey, Dave, I can hear him breathing. He's right there in front of you somewhere," I whispered just loud enough for Dave to hear.

"Yeah, I can hear him too. HOLY CROW! HE'S RIGHT THERE!" KABOOOM!

"Did you get him?" I asked after the echo of the shot died away in the distance.

"Yeah! He was in a hole right at my feet all the time I was standing here," he answered in a voice quavering with excitement.

I scrambled up through the alders and helped him drag the bear out onto the beach. While Dave field-dressed the carcass I went back for the skiff. Dave was pretty excited and the story got told quite a few times over the next few days. Next few years actually.

RICK'S BEAR

In the spring of the third year at Happy Harbor, Bob Bennett convinced me to turn my old plywood lifeboat into a handtroller and fish for salmon that summer. I figured that was an excellent idea, so I scrounged up a 16 horsepower Briggs & Stratton engine and installed it in the boat. I mounted cedar poles amidships to separate the lines, and made a pair of reels out of an old set of power trolling gurdies. The little double-ender was pretty cute all dressed up in her new green paint and her jaunty trolling poles.

It was around the first of June and I had two weeks to kill before the Coho season opened. I decided to putt up to Coal Bay and visit with Rex Arnce for a few days before I had to start fishing. Rex had wintered alone that year and I hadn't seen him since Christmas, so I was curious how he was doing.

When I arrived, he came down to the beach to admire my boat. After checking her out we went to the house and traded yarns about the winter over coffee. During the course of the conversation, Rex mentioned that his nephew, Rick, was living at Salt Chuck with his girlfriend, Anne, and their friend, John Lee. It was still early in the day and there are lots of hours of daylight that time of year. I suggested that we chug up in my boat and visit them for a day or two. Rex thought that was a great idea, so he grabbed his rifle and possible-sack and off we went.

It was a beautiful, sunny spring morning. Kasaan Mountain still had snow on its upper elevations, and it made a grand scene reflecting in the calm surface of the bay. There were a few puffy white clouds sailing on the ocean of blue sky, and the dark green hills were mirrored in the water.

About noon, as we approached the narrow entrance to the Chuck, Rex asked me how the trolling gear worked. I decided it would be easier to show him than to try to explain its complexities over the racket of the engine.

I lowered the pole on the starboard side, then lifted the eighteen-pound lead cannonball over the gunnel and lowered it just beneath the surface of the water. I took a leader out of the gear box and clipped it onto the trolling wire just above the lead. Next I snapped on a pale-blue trolling plug and flipped it into the water behind the boat. As it wiggled along seductively just beneath the surface, I released the brake on the gerdy reel and lowered it till it was about ten feet under water.

While we chugged on into the entrance of the lagoon I explained to Rex that if I were really fishing, I would continue to add lures to the line till the lead was just above the sea bottom. Then I would snap on the tag line from the end of the pole, and let the line out till it was dragging from the pole tip. I explained that the other line on the other side of the boat worked the same, and that while fishing, I would be towing both lines.

While we talked the boat was slowly pushing its way through the gut against the current. Suddenly, the line pulled way back! I panicked, thinking the lead was dragging on the bottom. I throttled up the engine, then reached across Rex and started cranking furiously on the gerdy handle. While I was trying to steer the boat and crank the reel, Rex was struggling to get out from under me in the narrow confines of the cockpit.

"Steer the boat, steer the boat!" I yelled as we tried to untangle ourselves. As we struggled, there was a great splash behind the boat and I saw a huge king salmon leap completely out of the water with the plug in his mouth.

"Steer the #$%# boat, we got a fish on!" I shouted again. Rex finally got a grip on the tiller and straightened the boat out in the current. The fish was yanking so hard on the leader that I had to give back line with the reel.

"Slow the engine down to an idle, we're going too fast!" I shouted, cranking back a few feet of line. The fish jumped out of the water again and fell back with a splash. We were gradually regaining control of the situation. Rex had the boat heading in the right direction, and the fish seemed to be tiring.

I continued to crank slowly, and when the leader broke the surface, I set the brake on the gerdy and looked around for my gaffhook. As I looked for it, I remembered that it was hanging in the shop at Happy Harbor. I had painted the handle and left it there to dry.

"I don't have a dang gaffhook! See if you can grab him behind the head when I pull him alongside," I said as I started to pull in the leader, hand over hand. The fish was worn-out and came quietly up to the stern of the boat. Rex let go the tiller and lunged for the fish, nearly capsizing the boat. The boat turned hard to starboard and the gunnel went under momentarily with Rex's weight. If I hadn't been hanging onto the gerdy stanchion I would have gone overboard.

Miraculously, he got a hold on the fish and it came aboard along with a big dollop of water. Rex threw his weight back the other way, and the fish went wild on the floorboards. It was about a twenty-five pound fish and it almost whipped us before we got it subdued. Rex pinned it to the deck while I whacked it between the eyes with a pipe wrench out of the toolbox.

We were both soaked with water and splattered with blood, but when the mist cleared, we had won. The boat was putting around in a tight circle with the rudder hard to starboard. I grabbed the tiller just in time to keep us off the beach, and pointed the bow on into the bay.

We looked at each other and busted out laughing. "That's how the gear works," I said, wiping the mess off my face with a sleeve.

"Next time bring the gaffhook; I don't think it's going to work landing them that way," Rex said with a chuckle.

I gutted the fish while Rex steered the boat toward the head of the bay. Half an hour later we nosed her up to the sand beach in front of the old superintendent's house at the mine. Rick and John came down to greet us, and when we had the boat secured we all went up to the house.

They had fixed the old place up to make a pretty comfortable camp. The house was built in the forties, during the last period of operation of the mine, and hadn't weathered the ravages of time very well. Abandoned buildings don't last very long in this country because of the high annual rainfall. Without heat and maintenance, they soon succumb to dry rot and dissolve into the ground.

This one had a metal roof and so had held up a little better. Rick and John had covered the windows with clear plastic and built a stove out of a steel oil drum. The furniture was made of scrap lumber and sections of logs, and cooking was done on a Coleman stove. Anne had a bouquet of salmonberry blossoms in a quart jar, which added a cheerful touch to the otherwise drab living space. They were happy in spite of the primitive living quarters, and were having a great adventure.

We yarned away the afternoon and eventually the subject of bears came up. Rick and John each had a new 7mm Magnum rifle and were anxious to shoot a bear. Neither had ever killed a bear before and they ask Rex and I to stay for a day or two and help them get one. We had no pressing engagements, so we agreed we would stay overnight and try a hunt in the morning.

We hung a target on an old piling out in the mud flat in front of the house, and sighted both rifles in to hit point of aim at 100 yards. Both guns had 3-9 variable scopes and we advised the boys to keep the power at the lowest setting. The cartridges they had were not much to my liking. The 140-grain factory loads are to high velocity, and the bullets are too light for bears at short range. The rifles were better suited to deer hunting in open country. The twenty-four inch barrels were unhandy in heavy timber, and the scopes were a detriment.

While we worked on the rifles, Anne fixed dinner: fresh king salmon steaks and boiled potatoes. After we had stuffed ourselves and told more stories, we turned in for the night.

We got up early and stoked up on hot cakes and coffee. When we were finished, we picked up our gear and went out into the cool, damp morning. We crossed the creek north of the shack and entered the woods. The trail cut across a point to Ellen Creek, which drained a series of big beaver ponds called Ellen Lake. The lake was about a half-mile off the beach. The creek ran between grassy banks down through an open meadow that varied from twenty to one hundred feet wide. There was a good run of dog salmon here in the fall, and lots of skunk cabbage and berries in the summer. It was prime bear country.

The trail passed through tall second-growth spruce and hemlock trees. The canopy of branches was so thick overhead that little light reached the forest floor. There wasn't much underbrush, so it was easy going and we made little sound as we slipped along the path.

It was about a quarter-mile across the point, and as we neared the creek we could see patches of bright green through openings between the tree trunks. We approached the edge of the timber carefully. Once in the open we would be able to see several hundred yards each way along the creek. There was a good chance that a bear would be feeding among the tender, spring grass shoots growing on the banks of the stream.

I was in the lead, and as I approached the edge of the trees I saw a large blue-black shape in the grass across the creek. I signaled the rest of the crew to stop while I crept closer. Standing in the grass across the creek was the biggest back bear I have ever seen! His black fur gleamed in the morning sun, jet black against the emerald green of the sedge grass. He was feeding contentedly in the morning sun and obviously was unaware of our presence.

I slipped back to the others and we discussed a plan. Rick and John wanted to give it a try and they decided Rick would fire the first shot. If a follow-up shot was necessary, John would shoot. Rex and the boys crept up to the edge of the woods, and while he coached them into shooting position, I moved upstream about fifteen yards to get a better view.

The bear was halfway between the creek and the timber on the other side of the stream. He was standing on a slope with his back toward Rick's position. The setup was perfect. Rick had a clear shot at the spine between the shoulders. The range was about forty yards and the bear was standing still, munching grass, when Rick fired.

The bear fell at the shot, then got up on its front feet and started dragging its hindquarters up the bank. John fired and the bear turned right and kept going parallel to the creek, moving very fast, dragging his hind-legs. He was heading toward a thicket of berry bushes and alder trees. I knew that if he got in there we were in trouble with a capital "T."

He was going past me from left to right at a range of about twenty yards. I stepped out into the open and shot him through the head between the eye and ear as he passed. He was dead before his chin hit the ground.

I stood there for a moment, stunned. You have to experience an event like this to fully understand it. There has been this gradual build-up of energy that accelerates to the moment of the animal's death. At that point, the energy flow into the event peaks and stops like turning off a switch. For a few heartbeats nothing moves: silence, time is frozen, total absence of energy flow.

Gradually my focus broadened from the bear to include the rest of the scene. Somewhere in the distance a raven called, and time started to move again. I looked toward Rick and John; they stepped out into the open and we grinned stupidly at each other. Rex walked out of the woods between us and crossed the creek to the bear. He approached it cautiously and jabbed it with his rifle barrel.

"Dead," he announced, visibly relaxing. I finally found my feet and crossed over to where he was standing by the bear.

"Nice shot," he said, looking me in the eye. Rick and John walked up and we examined the bullet wounds.

Rick's shot was centered but low. It struck right where the pelvis attaches to the spine. It broke the spine, severing the spinal cord, but did not penetrate on into the body cavity. John's bullet fragmented in the thick muscle in the right armpit. It made a nasty wound, but did not break the shoulder bone or penetrate into the rib cage. It didn't even knock the bear down, just turned him around to the right and headed him in another direction. The whole sequence happened so fast, neither of them had time to bolt another cartridge into the chambers of their rifles.

Once again, the importance of proper bullet placement, and matching the load to the game and local conditions, was driven home. The rifles had the energy to do the job, but it was improperly applied due to lack of knowledge and experience.

It is also important to have someone involved in the hunt with the experience to stay cool until the animal is anchored down for good. If I had not been there, that bear would have gotten into the brush and those kids would have been in a jam. Try to imagine two inexperienced young men, sneaking around in thick brush with their long-barreled, scoped rifles, trying to find that bear. Somebody would likely have gotten chewed. Or shot!

The tide was in, so I went for the boat while Rex helped them skin out their trophy. They were still at it when I came back. The bear was an enormous male, in the peak of his prime. I have never seen one bigger. He had three inches of fat covering his whole body under the hide. After the hide was off, we split the carcass into four quarters, and it was a grunt for one man to lift one of them into the boat. The hide was so heavy, it took two of us to load it.

Back at the house, we nailed the hide to the wall in the back bedroom so Rick and John could flesh it. The nose touched the ceiling and the rump was within an inch of the floor, on an eight-foot wall. We had no tape measure, but it must have squared around seven feet. They filled three five-gallon buckets with fat that they cut off the hide and meat.

Rex and I stayed one more night, then left at noon the next day when the tide was high. I talked to Rick in Ketchikan a few months later and he said that by the time they were through with the hide everything they owned was covered with bear grease. When they left for town a few days later they smelled so bad the pilot didn't want to let them on the plane. Rick didn't think he would be shooting any more bears for a while.

There was a funny story that made the rounds in the bay about that same time. There was a family who lived just outside the Salt Chuck who made their living logging. They lived on a float camp and had a big A-frame on a log raft with a donkey-winch to pull logs into the water. The A-frame had a stiff-leg to the beach to hold it offshore. Breast-lines angled off the corners of the raft to stumps ashore on either side of the stiff-leg. This held the raft in position and gave the men access to dry land.

One Sunday, while the crew was having a day off, the boss and one of the hired hands were over doing some maintenance work on the donkey engine. In the middle of the afternoon, one of the men looked up and saw a bear coming out the stiff-leg from the beach. The man's nickname was "Beaver" and he had quite a reputation around the logging community as a joker.

He decided to have some fun with the bear, so he picked up a sixteen-foot pike-pole and started out the stiff-leg toward the bear. They met in the middle of the log and were standing there like Robin Hood and Friar Tuck, trying to decide who had the right of way. The Beaver was holding the pike-pole at port arms and he and the bear were just standing there looking at each other. Poncho picked up a chainsaw and cranked the engine. The big saw fired up with a tearing sound that echoed off the mountain like the bellow of some great dragon.

From the bear's perspective the sounds seemed to come from behind him on the beach. He ran straight at Beaver and before the Beav' could bring his lance into play, the bear ran into him and they both fell into the bay. The bear swam out to the float and climbed aboard. Poncho ran down the stiff-leg to help Beaver out of the water and pulled him sputtering out onto the big spruce log.

Trouble was, now the bear was on the float and they were on the stiff-leg! The pike-pole had floated off and Poncho had left the chainsaw on the raft. They were stranded and weaponless. In a few minutes, the bear decided he better get back ashore, so he started down the stiff leg and the men had to hit the beach. The bear followed them ashore and disappeared into the woods. The men headed home to get the Beaver dried out and celebrate their adventure.

ACCIDENTAL BEAR

Salmon season ended in late September, and after being cooped-up on the boats all summer we were really feeling the itch to get into the woods. Deer season was open and the cedar ridges and muskegs were singing their siren call. October 1st rolled around and we had a spell of clear weather with a strong, north wind. It blew for several days, then one morning the wind was gone.

I tuned in the forecast while I enjoyed my morning coffee: light winds and clear skies for the next few days. This kind of weather is rare here that time of year, so I decided we better take advantage of it. I walked up the ramp from the dock where my little float house was tied, and knocked on Elden's door. Dave was there and Elden's brother, Karl.

"Lets go huntin'," I said as Elden poured me a cup of coffee. There were mumbles and nods of assent from all present and in a few minutes we had a plan. There was a slope on the south end of Kasaan peninsula that had always looked like good deer country. We fished offshore there during the summer and often saw deer on the beach. It was a difficult place to hunt because it was too far to go in the skiff, and there were no good anchorages along that part of the peninsula. However, with the calm weather that was forecast we figured we could anchor Elden's boat along the beach for a few hours while we hunted the hillside.

Elden threw together some flapjacks and fed us breakfast. When we were finished eating we scattered to our respective houses to round up our equipment. We finally had everything aboard the boat and untied the lines about 8:30. The water in Kasaan Bay was glassy-flat calm. The sun was still behind the peninsula to the east and the mountains, etched in black against the sunrise, were perfectly reflected in the mirror-like surface of the water.

It took about an hour and a half to run to the area that we wanted to hunt. We had the anchor down and set about 10:15. We rowed to the beach and anchored out the skiff so it would be afloat later when we came off the hill. After the rowboat was secured, we split up and started up the hill. Dave went off to the south, Elden and Karl went straight up the slope, and I angled off to the north.

I followed the game trail along the base of the mountain for a while, then took a trail that came down the hill on a cedar ridge between two tiny streams. My usual technique for hunting this type of country was to follow the deer trail up the slope till I found fresh sign. Then I would side-hill into the wind, hoping to jump one out of its bed.

The trail went up through a grove of ancient red cedars to a small bench at about three hundred-foot elevation. Above the bench the slope steepened considerably. The trees here were smaller and there were some spruce, hemlocks, and a few yellow cedars mixed in with the red cedars. There was little underbrush and aside from being steep, it was easy going.

Two hundred feet up was another narrow bench, and above that a steep slope rising to a third bench. I crossed the second bench, then climbed up to the third one. I was about eight hundred feet up the mountain and starting to feel the effects of the steep climb. There was a faint trail along the edge of the upper bench. It led to a tiny promontory, which looked like it would be a good spot to sit for a while to watch the trail below and catch my breath. I worked my way out onto the point and found a comfortable place to sit with my back to a tree, with the hill falling away at my feet.

It was beautiful there. The sun had come up over the ridge behind me and rays of light filtered down through the trees dappling the forest with patches of green and forming areas of deep shadow. A flock of small, brown birds flitted past, twittering to each other as they moved from tree to tree, looking for food. Somewhere below me a red squirrel was chattering furiously, and a raven croaked overhead. The place seemed full of life. As I sat soaking it all in, a Stellar's Jay landed on a dead limb over my head and announced to the world that I was there. He stayed for a few minutes, squawking and carrying on, then vanished up the hill.

I sat for about twenty minutes and was thinking about moving on up the hill when a flicker of movement caught my eye down on the bench below. I turned and looked at the spot but could see nothing. As I watched, a bear stepped out of the shadow, then walked over to the base of the slope.

He was about a hundred feet below my perch, and after standing there looking around for a moment, he started up the hill directly toward me. I could look straight down on him as he climbed up the steep slope, and I realized he was going to pass by about ten feet to my left. When he pulled himself up onto the bench he was so close I could have spit on him! Without thinking about what I was doing, I raised the little Marlin 30-30. I eared back the hammer and shot him right through the brain. The bear rolled back down the hill and fetched up under a rotten log at the bottom of the slope.

I levered another round into the chamber, set the hammer on half cock, then scrambled down to where he lay jammed under the log. I approached carefully and jabbed him with the rifle barrel to see if he was dead. As I stood there looking at him, a voice in my head said, "What the heck did you do that for, dummy; we were after deer meat, not bear meat."

The logistics of getting two hundred pounds of dead bear off that hill was not pleasing to contemplate. I gave myself a couple good swift kicks in the mental pants then laid the rifle down to start the onerous chore of field-dressing it.

The first task was to get the carcass out from under the log. There is not much for handholds on a bear, and when they are dead it's like trying to wrestle a two hundred-pound bag of Jell-O. I took hold of a hind leg and yanked on it. No luck. I climbed over the log and tried to push him back through the narrow gap where he was wedged. That didn't work either.

After several more fruitless attempts, I finally dug around him with my hands. It took a while, but eventually I got the corpse to slide on through the gap. When it broke free, it rolled down onto the bench and landed in a puddle of water. I picked up my rifle and climbed down to it.

After more pulling, pushing and shoving, I finally got him out of the muck and on his back so I could get the guts out. This would reduce the weight some and I realized I was going to need every advantage I could get. As I worked on the bear, I heard a shot echo off the mountain to the south.

When I finished gutting out the carcass, I cleaned myself up in the puddle and looked around for the best way down to the beach. To go the way I had come was out of the question. I would have to drag the bear uphill to get back on the trail and it was going to be hard enough to go downhill. I knew from having taken deer out of similar places that it was a mistake to go down a streambed, but I had no choice. I was already in the creek bottom and every direction was uphill except down the creek. It was not much of a stream, just a trickle, but I knew it would get worse as I went down the hill.

I slung the rifle across my back so I would have both hands free. I tried various purchases on the bear but it was almost impossible to get a decent grip on him. The legs were too thick, the head too big, and my hands couldn't grip the skin tight enough to hang on. I tried everything I could think of, but nothing worked. After about a half-hour of struggling, all I had succeeded in doing was moving the body about a hundred yards and wedging it under another log in the creek bottom.

I was sweating, out of breath, and covered with mud from head-to-foot. There was a cloud of blue smoke hanging in the air from the steady stream of cuss words I had been muttering, and there was not a bird or squirrel to be heard anywhere. It probably sounded like Godzilla-fighting-The-Creature-From-The-Black-Lagoon down in that crick bottom, and any critter with half a brain was long gone.

Finally, I cut through the soft tissue under the lower jaw and looped my belt through the jawbone. This gave me a better handle and I was able to drag him a little farther down the mountain. Unfortunately, I soon came to a steep drop where the creek spattered fifty feet down an almost vertical cliff to the next bench. It was uphill to everywhere again, so there was nothing I could do but shove him over and hope for the best. The bear rolled down the cliff like a bag full of blubber and ended up head down in a gully at the base of the hill.

As I lay there panting and cussing myself for being so stupid, I heard another shot off to the south. After I caught my breath, I staggered on down to the bear to try to free it from the latest obstacle. I struggled with it for about a half-an-hour and finally gave up. I was going to need help, so I better go see if I could find someone to give me a hand.

I climbed down the last slope to the bench above the beach, then down onto the trail along the shore. I soon stumbled out into the cove where the skiff was anchored. Karl and Elden were sitting on a log having a smoke, so I walked over and joined them.

I related my sad tale and we were just about to head back up the hill to rescue the bear, when Dave came out of the woods dragging a deer. He had shot the doe earlier in a small muskeg on the side of the mountain. As he was dragging it down the hill he had jumped a big buck and shot it also. He said he had been relaying them down the hill and had to go back to get the buck. When he was done he would come give us a hand with the bear.

Elden and Karl followed me back up to my trophy and the three of us soon had it headed down the mountain. Even with the three of us, it was no easy task and we were darn glad to see the bottom of the hill. Dave arrived at the skiff with his buck about the same time we got there. It took three trips to get the meat and ourselves out to the boat, but we were soon chugging up Kasaan Bay toward home. The meat would be welcome among the neighbors and we would have stories to tell during the long, dark, winter evenings.

There was another hunt along that same shore that almost ended in disaster. The next summer I bought a twenty-one foot boat in Ketchikan. It was set up for halibut fishing and handtrolling. Boots was down in the Lower 48 recuperating from surgery, and I was living in her cabin with my wife and our new son.

One nice, fall day I decided to run across to the peninsula in the big boat and hunt for a deer. I anchored the Nomad in a tiny, open cove and rowed the punt into the beach. I hunted up the side of Andrews Mountain, and about the time I got to timberline, I realized that the wind was coming up out of the south. The boat was anchored in a real bad spot for a southerly wind. I took off back down the mountain as fast as I could go. It took me about 45 minutes to work my way back down to the cove and when I arrived the boat was gone!

I stood there for a few moments with visions of the boat blown up on the rocks, ruined. Not only was it my only way home, it was our livelihood, and we still owed money on it. I was sick. The only thing I could think of to do was row out in the punt and see if I could see it. The bay was getting choppy and I didn't have much time before it got too rough for the tiny skiff.

I rowed out into the chop until I could see around the north point of the cove. The Nomad was about a mile up the beach and still not on the rocks. I figured that if I rowed like heck maybe I could catch her. The wind helped and I soon realized I was gaining on the boat. The chop was getting worse, and it was all I could do to keep the punt upright. It took me about 45 minutes to reach the Nomad, but I finally rowed around into the lee of the boat and climbed aboard.

Luckily the anchor had snagged in the rocky bottom before the boat washed up on the rocks. I soon had the engine running and the anchor aboard. As I ran across the bay toward home I realized that if I had not been able to row down to her I would have lost her. The wind was increasing and the big swells that came in off the Strait would have eventually swamped her, or chaffed off the anchor line and washed her up on the rocks. Lucked out again! You better believe I never anchored in a spot like that and left the boat again. It is amazing some of the dumb things a person does and gets away with it. It's a miracle that any of us live as long as we do. We're usually our own worst enemy.

BACKYARD BEAR

By the early 80s, the fishing around Kasaan Bay was getting pretty bleak. Bob Bennett and his family had sold out and moved back to Washington State. I was running out to Chatham Strait every summer. Fishing was still good around Port Alexander, on the southern tip of Baranof Island, and in 1981, single again, I decided to stay there year around. That fall I bought a thirty-foot gillnet boat and converted it into a troller. I lived aboard for the next few years, fishing out of PA in the summer and loafing around the dock in the winter.

Baranof Island had a good herd of deer and that was more interesting to me than the fishing. The only fly in the ointment was the fact that the island also had a large population of Alaska brown bears. These bears are second only to the Kodiak Island bears for size, and have a whole different personality than the black bears that inhabit Kasaan Bay. They can occasionally get as big as a thousand pounds and can be quite aggressive at times. Every year there are stories of unpleasant encounters between humans and these bears that often end in one or both parties getting hurt. Usually the bear.

There are usually bears lurking around the Port Alexander area, and it adds an element of excitement to deer hunting that most of us would rather do without. In the fall, after the fish runs are over, we often get to enjoy a bear or two prowling around town at night. They go from house-to-house, looking for a free meal, and it is not unusual for them to use the boardwalks anytime after dark.

One fall, there was a pair of three-year-old cubs working the grub line every night. They were coming onto people's porches in the evenings, or trying to get at deer that were hanging in woodsheds. It got worse as the fall progressed and food became harder to find. Finally, one night they ripped the door off Fred's shed and got a deer he had shot several days before. He decided enough was enough.

The next morning he came over to my boat and asked me to help him shoot one of them that night, if they came back. I agreed, so we borrowed a .458 magnum rifle from Jim Hendricks. We sighted it in on the beach south of town in the early afternoon, and after we were satisfied with the rifle, we rigged up bait in a tree in Fred's backyard. We hung a deer hide from a limb and smeared bacon fat and honey on it just for good measure.

The plan was to make a rest in the window of the upstairs bedroom and wire up a spotlight that shined on the hide. We hung some tin cans on the bait and when the cans rattled, Fred could flip on the light and shoot the bear. I would back him up with a 12 gauge pump shotgun if things didn't go as planned.

We had dinner and were sitting around the kitchen table telling bear stories. Around eight o'clock, Norman Pillen announced on the CB radio that a bear was trying to get into their rabbit cages. We figured there would be some action at our bait any minute. Fred went upstairs to his gun and I poked my shotgun out the kitchen window.

Five minutes later we heard the cans rattle. Fred flipped the switch on the spotlight and illuminated the scene. The bear was nosing the bait when the light hit him. We saw him for an instant, then he vanished into the darkness.

That was all the action that night. We stood watch the next evening also, but the bear didn't come back. The morning of the third day I decided to go home. I had work to do on the boat and it seemed, as the bears were gone.

That evening around eight o'clock I heard a loud rifle shot across the bay. Fred came on the CB radio a few minutes later and said he had shot the bear. It had run off into the dark and he couldn't see it. He thought he had made a killing shot through the chest, but didn't think it would be wise to go looking for it in the dark.

Next morning, he found it about fifty feet from the bait—stone dead. The whole episode caused quite a stir around town that day and almost everyone came for a look at the bear. The Department of Fish and Game came and took the skull and hide, but they eventually let the city of PA have it back. The city council had the skin tanned and made into a rug, and it still hangs on the wall at the community hall—which just happens to be called "Bear Hall."

By the time the bear was skinned and the carcass hauled off, the Pollard household had had about all the bear they could stand. The thing was rolling fat, and the meat had soured overnight from the body heat. Their house and yard stank of rotten bear for days and everything was covered with bear grease. We tried eating some of the meat, but it was so musky that it was completely unpalatable.

The next fall, Fred was deer hunting south of town and had shot a buck in a muskeg on the side of the mountain. He leaned his rifle against a bush and paunched out the deer. When he had the guts out, he dragged the deer to a small mound a few yards away, and propped it up to let the blood drain out of the body cavity.

When he looked up, a bear was coming toward him. The rifle was about halfway between Fred and the bear, and he knew he didn't have a chance to reach it. There was a clump of cedars to Fred's left. He stepped behind the nearest one and yanked out the Ruger .22 automatic pistol he was carrying in a belt holster.

As he moved behind the tree, the bear changed course and came right over to where Fred was hiding. Fred fired several shots into the air. The bear turned around in his tracks, ran back the other way, then disappeared into the woods. Fred was pretty shaken. He grabbed his rifle and the deer and hotfooted it for the beach, looking over his shoulder all the way.

The next day he ordered a brand new Ruger Red Hawk .44 magnum pistol. I couldn't stand it, so I ordered one too. This began a period of experimentation with loads, holsters, and carrying techniques that lasted several years.

We tried everything we could think of. We experimented with all of the bullets available from the reloading suppliers, then moved on to cast bullets. We did penetration tests in various mediums, and tried all the different powder types we could lay our hands on. We eventually settled on a 300-grain hard-cast bullet, loaded as hot as the guns would stand. It was pretty brutal to shoot, but gave impressive penetration in every medium into which we shot them.

I bought a Dillon progressive reloading tool, and we made up a mild practice load, using scrap lead bullets. We were able to shoot cheaply and by recovering the lead, then recasting it into new bullets, we could practice often. Finally, we figured we were ready for bear. When spring came, we decided to shoot a black bear to see if our loads worked on the real thing.

One fine, April day, Fred, his wife Melanie, their two kids and I piled into Fred's boat, the Kim. We ran across Chatham Strait to Port Malmsbury, on Kuiu Island. We anchored in a bay called the Mud Hole that night and saw the first bear that evening.

We spent the next couple days idling the boat around the area looking at bears. There were several feeding on the beaches every day, and we finally decided on a big male with mud on his hind legs. The kids called him "the dirty pants bear," and we saw him every afternoon as he gradually drifted toward the end of the east arm of Port Malmsbury.

One afternoon, we realized the bear would go around a point in about an hour. The wind would be perfect to go ashore on the other side of the point and set up an ambush. We anchored the boat near the head of the bay and Fred, Jack, and I rowed into the beach behind the point. There was a tiny cove there, so we hid the skiff just to the east of it.

When the skiff was secure, we walked to the point opposite the one the bear would come around. Fred sat under a big red cedar with his back against the trunk and his elbows on his knees. This gave him a steady rest for a two-handed grip on the big pistol. Jack hid behind the tree, and I found a spot a few yards inside the edge of the timber, where I had a clear view around my stand. We figured if the bear was wounded he would go for the woods, and I would be waiting with my Marlin 45-70.

It seemed like a long time passed and I had almost decided that the bear wasn't going to show. Suddenly I heard a scraping noise and the bear appeared on the beach, coming around the point. It was fifty yards away, walking toward Fred. It stopped at about thirty-five yards and turned over several large stones looking for crabs to eat. It snuffled around for a while, then walked on toward Fred.

BLAM... the bear went down and I saw the bullet splash in the bay about fifty yards form the shore. The bear got back up onto its feet and headed toward Fred. BLAM... the bear went down again and I saw another splash offshore. The bear got to its feet again and disappeared behind a tree that blocked my view of the beach. BLAM...the bear fell into view again, then got back to its feet. Fred fired a fourth shot and it went down again.

While all this was happening, I was trying to keep a sight-picture on the bear in case I needed to shoot. After the fourth shot, it got back to its feet and headed on toward Fred. I couldn't see Fred from my position because there was a big cedar in the way. The bear was only about twenty feet from Fred and still on its feet. It would soon disappear behind the tree and if I didn't shoot now, I would lose sight of the bear.

I took a bead on the neck and pulled the trigger. KA-BOOOMM, the big forty-five caliber rifle fired. The bear went down and I saw the bullet splash in the water out in the cove. I levered another cartridge into the chamber and put the front bead on the bear's head. It didn't move, and in a moment Fred walked into view pointing the

.44 at it. I uncocked the Marlin and walked down to the beach. Fred reloaded the chambers in the big revolver and shoved it in his holster.

"Why did ya shoot? I'd have had him on the next shot," he said, rolling the bear over on its side so he could examine the bullet wounds. I was taken aback.

I stood there looking at him for a moment. "Didn't look to me like you had him; he was back on his feet after taking four bullets and I was about to lose sight of him. If you want me to back you up, I'll decide when it's time to shoot. Find someone else next time." It was the beginning of the end of our friendship. The rest of the trip was miserable. We tried to be civil to each other, but finally just resorted to silence.

Three of the pistol bullets had hit the front shoulder and passed completely through the body, exiting just ahead of the hindquarter on the other side. The fourth went through one of the front legs. None of them hit the shoulder bone or any other major bone structures. All three that passed through the body would have been fatal eventually, but I still believe you need to break the spine forward of the front shoulders as soon as possible. Sever the spinal cord and everything from that point back shuts down instantly.

The 350-grain Hornady round-nose from my 45-70 destroyed a section of spine about four inches long, between the shoulders and the skull. If any of those .44 bullets had hit the spine, the bear would have died instantly. The .44 has plenty of power, but bullet placement is the most important factor. I think, however, that most of the 240-grain factory loads are too soft to get reliable penetration on a bear. Especially the hollow points that so many people think are the ultimate bullets. There is no substitute for tough bullets and proper placement.

I packed that big, heavy pistol around for several years, but never had occasion to use it. It was usually inaccessible under a coat and the weight became an awkward burden after while. I finally sold it to one of my friends who was as bad a gun nut as I was. Occasionally I regret letting it go, but not bad enough to buy another one. Not yet anyway.

CLOSE ENCOUNTERS

One fall, I was offered a chance to live ashore in a tiny, two-room house along the main boardwalk in Port Alexander. It was a pretty funky old shack, drafty and hard to heat, but I was ready for a winter off the boat. I moved in October and spent several weeks tidying the place up and making it livable. The best part was that I could sneak out the back door anytime with the rifle, and after a short walk, I was in the woods.

I really enjoy hiking around through the forest, so I began taking a tour of the area east of town every day. I would cross the small bay behind my house, then head into the timber. Over time, I worked out a route that I followed. I gradually discovered all the main deer trails, where the beds were located, and when they were being used. I learned that certain weather conditions would influence the deer's choice of beds and feeding areas. This gave me the information I needed to find one if I needed meat.

I also discovered that the animals in the area became accustomed to my presence, and my scent became part of the background. As long as I stayed on my regular route, they could avoid me, but would not leave the area. I tried several experiments and found that by varying my route I could surprise them either in their beds or feeding grounds. It was fun and enlightening, and also provided me with meat when I needed it.

Several bears also used this area, and from time to time one of them would pass through and hang out for a few days. In the fall after the fish are gone, they spend most of their time scavenging the southern beaches for dead sea life and sandfleas. They will also take a deer if they get a chance. Some bears actually become quite adept at lurking on the deer trails and pouncing on them as they pass. This adds quite an element of excitement to deer hunting in brown bear country.

My daily route took me up along a ridge behind town, then down onto the beach in a tiny bay we called Judy's Cove. It was a beautiful place with a crescent of gravel beach in the back and piles of driftwood to poke round in. The main deer trail, from the muskegs above the bay, crossed this beach, and every morning there were fresh tracks in the gravel. It was also a favorite sandflea digging spot for the bears. Sandfleas are tiny, shrimp-like critters that live in the gravel on the beach, and the bears love them. They will spend days rooting in the gravel and driftwood piles, licking the fleas up as they try to escape.

One morning I realized there were no fresh deer tracks on the beach. It didn't make much of an impression on me at the time, and after resting on a log for a while enjoying the winter sun, I went on my way. The next day there was still a conspicuous absence of fresh tracks. My mind was on other things, so I didn't give it much thought.

On the third day, I decided to use a different route into the cove. I had been approaching along the shore every morning, but this day I came over the point between town and Judy's Cove. The trail came down off the hill on the West Side of the cove, about halfway to the gravel beach, then followed the shoreline just inside the trees. The timber was open and the ground was covered with knee-high sedge grass.

The trail passed all the way around the bay, but I decided to go out onto the beach and check for tracks. It was about ten yards from the trail to the beach. As I went around a big spruce tree, I noticed that the grass was flattened-out and the ground had been dug up in a circle, about eight feet in diameter. As I looked around, I saw a white object sticking out of the dirt, so I reached down and pulled it free.

It was a splinter of deer bone with shreds of meat still attached.... I looked down and saw more pieces of bone and tissue half-buried in the dirt and grass. Suddenly, I realized that I was standing on a fresh kill that a bear had buried.

I dropped the bone and eared back the hammer on the Marlin. The hair was standing up on the back of my neck, and I could feel a powerful presence. The kill was only a day or two old and there was plenty of meat left. I could feel the bear there in the brush, and every sense was screaming at me to get the heck out of there as quick as I could. Bears will sometimes fight tooth-and-claw to protect a kill.

I held the rifle ready and backed slowly out onto the beach. When I was clear of the timber, I beat feet back to town fast as I could. I was pretty spooked. I knew the bear was right there watching me. It was just luck that it didn't come tearing out of the bushes while I was standing there trying to figure out what I was looking at. I wouldn't have had a chance to shoot before he was on me. As I headed for home, I realized that I had been passing within a few feet of the kill as I walked the beach into the cove each morning.

I stayed out of Judy's Cove for a while. When I finally went back, there was no fresh bear sign in the area. The kill was still visible and had obviously been fed on after I was there, but hadn't been disturbed for quite a while. One thing that jumped right out at me was that the log I had rested on the two days prior to finding the kill was only about fifteen feet from the buried deer carcass. It's a miracle I didn't get jumped on one of those days.

I had a similar encounter about a year later within a few hundred yards of Judy's Cove. One afternoon I had been rambling around in the hills east of town and was headed home. I came down off the north ridge and crossed the beach in the back of the cove. There were several pits dug in the gravel on the East Side of the cove, sure sign that a bear was around.

I decided to take a shortcut over the hill on the West Side of the bay and entered the woods right about where the bear had made his kill the previous fall. I followed a deer trail up onto the low ridge, and when I got to the top of the hill, there were very fresh deer tracks in the trail. I was ready for some venison, so I decided I would blow the deer call several times to see if I could call one out into the open. It was almost dark, but I was close to home and figured I had about a half-hour.

I took a stand were I could see along the trail for a couple hundred feet and blew the call several times. A few minutes later I called again, and as the echoes of the call faded I heard gravel crunching down on the beach in the back of Judy's Cove. I waited a while but heard nothing more. It was rapidly getting dark and I decided I was out of time, so I went on home.

The next two days were wet and stormy, so I stayed home. I loafed around the house, reading and visiting with the neighbors. By the third day, the weather had cleared and I was getting restless. I went back up onto the muskegs behind town early in the morning, hoping to see a deer. I hunted through the morning and into the early afternoon without success. I decided to go down through Judy's Cove on the way home, to see if the deer was still hanging around on the hill between the cove and town.

There were bear tracks on the beach and more sandflea excavations. It was getting late so I didn't hang around long. I went back into the woods on the trail over the hill to the west and headed for home. As I followed the faint path through the cedar grove on the hilltop, I noticed that there were no fresh deer tracks, even in places that were sheltered from the recent rain. I soon topped out on the ridge and followed it as it curved around toward town.

One section of the trail goes along the top of a steep bank that drops about fifty feet into a brush-choked bowl. There is a tiny cove with a small gravel beach just beyond the thicket. I came over the top of the hill and turned to follow the path at the top of the bank.

Suddenly I heard something go crashing down the cliff through the brush and out onto the beach! I thought it was a deer, and was kicking myself in the mental pants for not being more quiet. I glanced down at the path to look for tracks and discovered that I was standing on the remains of a deer that was partially buried in the trail.

Once again, the hair stood up on the back of my neck, and my thumb eared back the hammer on the Marlin. Fortunately for me, the bear had heard me coming and decided to flee. If I had been sneaking down the trail looking for deer, I might have tripped over him. Lucked out again…

One spring we were having a spell of nice weather in early April. It had been calm and clear for several days and the forecast was for more of the same. My friends, Marty and his wife, Jean, asked me if I would like to go with them up the outside coast of Baranof Island to explore some of the bays out there. I thought it was a great idea, so we loaded a few necessities of life into their boat and headed for Cape Ommaney.

The ocean was flat calm and the sun shined everyday. We had an enjoyable adventure in one of the wildest places in the world. This area is rarely accessible because of the weather and big seas along this coast. We felt lucky to be able to enjoy it for a few days under such perfect conditions.

The last day out, we were passing a small inlet just north of Cape Ommaney, called Little Puffin Bay. It is a shallow cove in a basin with steep cliffs towering a thousand feet on either side. The mouth of the bay is exposed to the open sea, and the big southwest swells roll right to the head to crash on a crescent-shaped, gravel beach.

There is usually so much surge on this beach that it is impossible to get ashore here, but because of the extended period of calm weather we had been enjoying, the surge looked manageable. We anchored the Dorothy Ann in the back of the bay and went ashore in the skiff.

It was a wild, magnificent place. There were great piles of stones that had been rolled in the surf until they were rubbed round. The gravel came in all sizes, from boulders a foot in diameter, to patches of fine green sand. Above the beach, at the foot of the cliffs, there was a small patch of woods made up of giant, old Sitka spruce and western hemlock trees. The forest floor was mostly free of underbrush, and was covered with a soft, green carpet of moss. It was a magical place; like an elf forest out of some fairy tale.

On the West Side, there was a creek tumbling over moss-covered boulders. It came out of a steep-sided gorge that disappeared upward between two cliffs. Along its banks were piles of fish bones, where bears had been feeding during the fall salmon run.

Just east of the creek was a great disk-shaped slab of rock that had come down off the mountain in some ancient upheaval. It was thirty feet in diameter, ten feet thick, and was buried edgewise in the ground, creating an overhang big enough to stand up under. There were the remains of several deer that had been killed and eaten by a bear in recent months. As we looked around under the rock, we realized that there were hundreds of deer bones and masses of hair mixed with dirt and rotten wood.

There was a trail coming down off the mountain that passed under the edge of the rock slab. On one side of the path, the remains of a tree stump provided a perfect place for a bear to lie in wait for a deer to come down the hill. This ambush spot had obviously been used for hundreds of years, and the more we looked around, the more deer remains we found. There were five kills that had been made that winter and signs of at least three different bears. There was an eerie feeling there—like being in someone's house when they are not at home.

We explored for a couple hours, then rowed back out to the boat and headed for home. I have always wanted to return to the bay and follow the trail up the gorge; it must lead to some excellent deer country that has probably never been hunted by humans. But then, maybe I won't; perhaps it's good to leave a few places untouched.

One of my personal rules is to not go wandering around in bear country unarmed. I rarely break that rule, but I remember one time I did break it, and ended up regretting it.

It was mid-March and the weather had been wet for weeks. Finally, a spell of dry weather came along and the warm sun was a welcome change from the late, winter storms that had been pounding the coast.

One Saturday morning, my wife, Mim, and I decided to take a walk east of town to enjoy the nice weather. For some reason, I decided to leave my rifle home. We rowed across the harbor to the front dock and left the skiff on the skiff float. We walked up the main boardwalk to Woody Avenue, then struck off through the trees for Judy's Cove. It took us about an hour to work our way through the timber, then along the beach to the cove. When we arrived at Judy's cove, we sat on a big driftwood log for a while to rest and enjoy the view.

Looking south, we could see Wooden Island at Cape Ommaney, and off on the horizon we could just barely make out the Hazy Islands. We sat on the log for about a half-hour, then walked on east around the next point and found a sunny spot to eat lunch.

We loafed around for an hour or so, nibbling food and poking around in the piles of driftwood that the winter storms had deposited on the shore. At one point, I vaguely remember hearing some sounds back in Judy's Cove, but it didn't really capture my attention. Around three o'clock, the sun had moved around to the west and our picnic spot became shaded by the big spruces along the beach. We packed up our daypacks and started for home.

As we worked our way along the east shore of Judy's Cove, Mim spotted an interesting bird in a big old hemlock tree and was watching it with the binoculars, trying to identify it. I was poking around in a big pile of driftwood logs, about twenty-five yards from where the crescent of gravel beach started in the head of the cove.

I had climbed up over the pile of logs and was standing facing east with the gravel beach to my left. There was a clump of alder brush hanging out between the East End of the beach and the spot where I was standing. I remember seeing a brown hump on the other side of the alders, but I was occupied beachcombing and it didn't really get my attention.

I glanced over at Mim just as she looked my way. Suddenly, she got a shocked look on her face and mouthed, "BEAR!" She pointed past me at the alders to my left. I turned to look just in time to see an enormous bear walk out onto the gravel. He was standing right beside the log that we had rested on earlier, sniffing at a pile of kelp at his feet. He was so close that I could see twigs stuck in the hair of his belly. I slowly moved over to where Mim was standing, and we walked slowly back the way we had come, glancing back at the bear frequently to see if he was following us. I don't think the bear was ever aware of our presence. The wind was from him to us, and he was quartering away so we weren't in his line of sight.

We circled around through the woods above the bay to avoid him. It was a long walk and I was kicking myself all the way for leaving the gun home. It's a miracle that I didn't walk around that bush and run right into him. Because of the layout of the shoreline, I would have had him cornered with his back to a bluff. We would have both been surprised and anything could have happened.

I recognized the bear; he was a big, old, mature male that I had seen several times over the years. He stood about chest-high at the shoulders and probably weighed somewhere between eight hundred and a thousand pounds. He is definitely the dominate male in the area and isn't afraid of anything. I have measured his tracks in mud and his front foot is about eleven inches wide. Too big to wrestle!

PART II

DEER TRAILS

CHRISTMAS BUCK

It was the day after Christmas. There had been a series of storms blowing in off the Pacific Ocean for several weeks. The deep low-pressure systems had brought warmer temperatures, rain, and strong southeast wind. The snow that had fallen in late November had melted, leaving the landscape a mixture of drab grays, greens, and browns. The last front had passed through late in the afternoon on Christmas Day and the wind had switched to the southwest. The sun had appeared through breaks in the clouds just before it set behind the mountains to the west and you could feel the air cooling. During the night the temperature fell below freezing for the first time in three weeks, and a series of westerly squalls passed by while the world slept, dropping several inches of new snow.

    I woke up just before daylight to the sound of wind rattling through the spruces outside. I looked out the door and it was snowing furiously. I put the coffee water on to boil, then turned on the radio to see if the world had ended yet. I also wanted to listen to the weather forecast; it was the last day of deer season and we were out of meat.

    As the coffee came to a boil, I realized that the wind had died away. I poured a cup and looked outside again. It had stopped snowing and I could see a few stars to the west. The weather forecast was just coming on the radio, so I turned up the volume and listened carefully while I sipped my coffee.

"High pressure will build in from the north bringing clearing skies and colder temperatures. Winds northwest fifteen today, changing to northeast twenty tomorrow. Outlook, northeast thirty with heavy, freezing spray," the announcer chanted in the peculiar droning voice that they use to give the forecast. It sounded like a good day to hunt. The cold weather and snow would have the deer moving, and I would be able to cross from the island to Kasaan Peninsula in the skiff.

I cooked a pan of rolled oats with raisins and brown sugar for breakfast, and made a sandwich for lunch. After breakfast, I assembled my gear and headed down to the dock. As I crunched through the new snow, the first faint light of dawn was turning the eastern sky a pale yellow. I brushed the fluffy snow off the skiff seat and cranked the outboard to reluctant life. When it was warmed up enough to idle smoothly, I untied the lines and headed for the harbor entrance. Outside the harbor, Kasaan Bay was flat calm. The light increased gradually and the mountains turned a silver blue as the morning light reflected off the new snow.

It is about two miles from Happy Harbor across the bay to Kasaan Peninsula. By the time I arrived in the tiny bay where I intended to hunt, there was enough light to see fresh tracks in the snow above the tide line.

The tide was out, so I uncoiled a line up the beach and tied it to a tree limb. I went back down and put a large stone on the anchor line, so the boat would stay off the beach as the tide returned. When the boat was all set, I took my rifle and day pack and headed for the woods.

There were many tracks in the snow above the high tide line. After studying them for a few minutes, I could see that a small band of does and a large buck had nibbled alder buds and pawed through the snow for kelp not long before my arrival. It had snowed just before daylight and they had been here after the last squall had passed, probably while I was eating breakfast!

I followed the tracks into the woods, then along a trail that paralleled the beach for a short distance to the south. The tracks soon turned uphill and I followed them quietly through a grove of giant old-growth spruce and hemlock trees. There was little underbrush and the trail was easy to follow, even though not much snow had made it to the ground through the thick canopy of limbs overhead.

It was a beautiful morning on that mountainside among those ancient trees. The sunlight filtered down through the limbs overhead, and the air was so cold and full of oxygen that it was almost too rich to breathe. As I climbed, I could hear ravens calling somewhere in the distance, and a flock of chickadees flitted through the branches overhead.

The mountain rose to the east in a series of steep slopes, with narrow benches every few hundred feet. The tracks climbed up onto the first bench, then turned south for a few hundred yards. They soon went uphill again, then followed the next bench farther to the south. This pattern repeated several times up and south, until it eventually turned east and crossed a shoulder of Kasaan Mountain.

There was a low pass between Kasaan Mountain and the next hill to the south, and the trail came out of the timber into a series of small muskeg meadows. I was moving very slowly, thinking I would find the deer bedded down at any moment.

The sun was already clear around into the southwest. The days are really short that time of year and the shadows were already lengthening into late afternoon. I checked my watch and was surprised to find that it was already 2:15 PM. It would be black-dark by four-thirty and I was a long way from the skiff. The last thing I wanted to do was spend the night in the woods in freezing weather in wet clothes. I decided to follow the tracks for another half-hour. If I didn't find him I would head back to the boat.

I continued slowly out into the open and stopped to look around. Suddenly, the buck stood up about forty yards away! He had been lying under the branches of a small cedar tree, watching his back trail. Without considering the lateness of the hour or the distance back to the boat, I raised the 47-70 and put a 300-grain bullet through his head.

I levered another cartridge into the chamber, then walked over to where he lay. As I stood there looking at him, I heard another deer make a whistling snort and bound away. I looked at my watch; it was 2:45 and I had a lot of work to do.

I field-dressed the deer, then toggled the front feet through the tendons on the back legs, to make a pack out of it. When it was ready, I dragged the carcass to a hump in the muskeg and tipped it onto my back with my arms under the front legs. It was a heavy load, but in those days I had more brawn than brain, so I figured I could manage it. Packing it would be faster than dragging it, and I didn't have much time before dark.

I picked up my rifle from where it was leaning against a bush and started back down the mountain. I did okay for a couple hundred yards until I stepped over a fallen tree into an ankle deep mud hole. When I tried to pull my foot out of the mud, my boot came off. So there I am, one boot stuck in the mud, standing in my sock in the snow, with the deer on my back. I knew if I put the deer down to retrieve my boot that I would never be able to pick it up again. I tried to wiggle my foot back into the boot, but all I managed to do was fall over, drop the deer, and sit down in the mud hole.

Time was running out fast; the light was fading and I was really wet now. I pulled the boot out of the mud and yanked it on my foot. I picked up the rifle, grabbed the deer by the horn, and took off down the hill as fast as I could go.

It was getting dark rapidly, so I figured I better go straight down to the beach. I knew I would come out too far south, but decided it would be easier to make my way along the beach in the dark than through the woods. Unfortunately, the direct route lead me down into a creek bottom that soon turned into a steep-walled gorge.

I was really wet now. The creek was full of fallen logs, and I was sweating from every pore as I struggled to wrestle the carcass over one log and under the next. I soon realized that I was not going to make it to the beach with the deer before dark, and spending the night in the woods was out of the question. It would be tough enough in dry clothes, but wet as I was, I would freeze solid by morning.

I decided the best thing to do was leave the deer and head for home. I could come back in the morning to finish dragging it to the beach. I draped the carcass over a log and covered it with some half-rotten limbs, hoping to protect it from the ravens until I could get back for it the next day.

I scrambled on down the creek bed in the fading light and eventually stumbled out onto the beach. There was only a faint glow in the sky to the west. I was a half-mile south of the skiff, and I soon discovered that the tide was too high to walk the beach. There was a fifty-foot cliff that fell straight into the water between the small cove and me where the skiff was anchored.

I had to go back into the nearly pitch-black woods, climb up over the bluff, and down into the other bay. It was a nightmare. I don't remember how many times I fell. Much of the way I traveled on my hands and knees, feeling ahead with my hands. I was afraid I would walk off into a hole and injure myself too badly to travel. Eventually I stumbled out onto the shore of the cove, and there was the boat, bobbing happily out in the bay. I pulled her in and took off for home.

The old house looked mighty good with smoke coming out of the chimney and the warm glow of a kerosene lamp in the kitchen window. I was hungry, half-frozen, and real glad to be home.

I went back in the morning and retrieved the buck in good condition. The meat is long gone, but the memory lives. Nowadays, I carry a small flashlight in my pocket. You never know when something that simple might be the difference between life and death.

I had one other close call that winter that almost won me a night on the beach. I had gone around the West Side of Kasaan Island to hunt a series of meadows just south of Hundred Thousand Creek. It was a cold February day with a frigid north wind that cut through your clothes like a knife.

I anchored the skiff off a small, gravel beach in a tiny cove that was sheltered from the wind. I hunted a big circle through the timber and back down through the meadows to the cove where I had left the boat. I saw two sets of tracks, but nothing alive. The woods had a late-winter dead feel, and it was so cold I had to keep moving to keep warm.

The tide had come in while I was in the woods and the skiff was floating about fifty feet out from the edge of the water. I laid my rifle on my daypack and took hold of the anchor line to pull in the skiff. The line was tied to a fifteen-pound lead ball with an eye cast in it, and there was about fifteen feet of line between the lead ball and the bow of the boat. When I pulled on the line between the anchor and the shore, the anchor hung up momentarily, and when I yanked on it to pull it loose, the rope broke!

I pulled in the rest of the line and inspected the end. It had chafed through, just shoreward of the knot where it was tied to the anchor. I looked out at the skiff. It was twenty feet from the edge of the water, and might as well have been two hundred feet. The air temperature was about twenty degrees, and the water temperature was just barely above freezing. Far too cold to swim out to the boat. I couldn't swim anyway, so it was pointless to consider.

I had one thing going for me. The tide was just about to change, and in about six hours the water would be out far enough so I could reach the skiff. I had matches and a sheath knife in my pack, so I could make a fire and wait it out.

It was getting on toward dark and the wind seemed to be increasing. I knew if it got much stronger I wouldn't be able to make the crossing to Kasaan Island, and I sure didn't want to do it in the dark.

Also, if the wind got too strong to cross the narrow channel, it might be days before it laid down enough for me to cross. I figured I better try to get the boat. If nothing else, it would give me something to do while I waited for the tide to go out.

I walked along the beach for a short distance in both directions looking for a pole long enough to reach the boat, but there was nothing that would serve. The only other plan I could come up with was to tie a rock on the piece of line I had and see if I could throw it into the boat. Maybe it would hang up on something and I could drag the skiff in where I could reach it.

Rocks were scarce, but I finally found a cylindrical one in the mouth of a creek. It weighed about seven or eight pounds and was shaped about right for tying on the rope. When I had it lashed to the end of the line, I coiled the rope carefully in my left hand. I swung the rock around several times with my right hand and let her go. The rock sailed over the bow of the skiff, but the weight turned it toward me and the line fell off. I pulled it in and tried again. This time the rock fell short, but it went across the anchor line, between the boat and the anchor. I pulled carefully and felt it snag on the other line.

The anchor came a few feet up the beach, then my rock slipped off again. I pulled in the rock and tried again. This time I was able to get it within about ten feet of the beach before the stone slipped loose. The third time, I threw the rock into the stern of the skiff and pulled it around toward me. By wading out to the tops of my boots, I could just barely reach the transom and was able to pull the boat in close enough to get in. Whew! Lucked out again.

I pulled in the anchor and fired up the motor. After retrieving my pack and rifle, I headed for home, thankful not to be hunkered over a smoky fire, freezing on one side and cooking on the other, trying to keep warm. The wind did pick up overnight; I would have been stranded for several days if I had been unable to retrieve the skiff.

One of the neighbors also had a close call that winter. Hank Hamer, and his wife, Arlie, lived in a log cabin on the west side of

Happy Harbor. Hank was retired from the state ferries and they were enjoying their retirement, living a wilderness lifestyle. Every winter he supplemented his retirement checks by trapping otter, marten, and mink around the bay. Henry was an experienced woodsman and did quite well with his trapline every winter. He had a sixteen-foot aluminum skiff and made a circuit of the bay every day, when the weather permitted.

One afternoon Mrs. Hamer rowed over to my place about an hour before dark and said that Hank was overdue from running his traps. I gathered up two guys from Bob Bennett's place and we went out in my troller to see if we could find him.

We headed north when we left the harbor. When we cleared the entrance, I could see a fire on Round Island, just north of Kasaan Island, about three miles from the harbor entrance. We found Hank's skiff about a mile south of Round Island, drifting along with its anchor on the bow, and the anchor line trailing along behind. We grabbed the skiff as we passed and a few minutes later we found Hank, hunkered by a fire on the south shore of Round Island. He was pretty glad to see us and as we motored home he told us his story.

He had otter sets on the island and was going ashore to check them. There are no beaches on Round Island and he usually anchored the skiff off a ledge on the south side. He would put the anchor on the bow and shove the skiff out, paying out line until it was out far enough, then yank the anchor off the bow. He would tie the line to a limb and go check his traps.

That day, when he had pushed the skiff out, he had slipped and fallen face down in the water. He had let go the line and the skiff had floated away while he floundered around trying to get back to his feet. His foot had wedged in a crack in the rocks and he was trapped. He could just barely keep his face above water by putting both hands on the bottom and arching his back. He said he about froze trying to get his foot free and almost panicked when he realized the tide was still flooding. It took about three minutes to get his foot out of the crack and by the time he finally got loose, the boat was out of reach.

Luckily, he had thrown his trapping bag up on the ledge before he tried to anchor the skiff. He had a hatchet in the bag and a container of waterproof matches. The first thing he did was strip and wring the water out of his wool clothing, then he got a fire going where he figured we would see it when we came looking.

Henry was no fool; he had the right equipment along and good wool clothing, which will keep you somewhat warm, even if it is wet. These kinds of accidents happen to everybody eventually if you spend enough time in the wild. Luck favors the prepared mind.

LOST

*P*OP! SSSSSssssss. A pocket of steam bursts in a chunk of cedar deep in the fire. A red-hot ember arcs off into the night, like a tracer bullet. Startled, my mind jumps back into the moment. I pick up a stick and push the burned ends of the driftwood pieces into the heart of the fire. It flares back into flame, illuminating the cedar bough lean-to behind me. The circle of light touches the black water of Smith Lagoon a few feet beyond the fire. I look around into the darkness, and a loon calls somewhere off in the distance. I refill my deer horn pipe and light it with the burning end of the stick. As I sip smoke through the stem, made of a goose's wing bone, my gaze drifts back into the flames. The hypnotic colors and movements soon lull me back into dreamtime.

My mind runs one more time through the tape of the day's wanderings that have brought me to this lonely camp on the wrong side of Scowl Point. I should be in Herring Cove, on the Kasaan Bay side of the peninsula, where my friends are probably waiting out the night wondering what has happened to me.

We left home before dawn to hunt the muskegs above Herring Cove. It is a favorite place where we have often hunted, a pass across a peninsula between Kasaan Bay and Scowl Arm. There is an old mossy-horn buck that rules the area. We have been trying to outsmart him for several years but have never seen him. Only his tracks and horn rubs.

We left the beach at first light. Dave went up the mountain to the north, Elden and his brother Karl up to the south. My plan was to hunt up the shoulder of the mountain to the north, which steps upward in a series of wide benches. These benches are timbered with small cedars and there are muskeg meadows scattered among the trees. I had hunted here before with good success and knew the old buck cruised that area in the fall until the snow came.

I followed the creek at the head of the bay toward its headwaters in the pass. After a climb of about a hundred feet up a narrow gorge, I came out into a meadow with a small beaver pond in the middle. The meadow was surrounded with tall, old growth spruce and hemlock timber. I intended to move slowly upstream to the summit of the pass, then hunt up the ridge to the north.

I followed the south shore of the pond to its head, then turned left into another meadow with a larger pond. At the head of this pond, I crossed the creek and pushed through a narrow band of small yellow cedar trees into another clearing with a third pond. I followed along the north shore of the third beaver pond, then climbed a couple hundred feet up a timbered slope into the pass. The drainage on the Kasaan Bay, or east, side of the pass funnels down this series of ponds and empties into Herring Cove.

The pass was quite wide and to the west were several drainages that flowed into Smith Lagoon, a salt chuck in the back of Smith Cove in Skowl Arm. The view from the pass was spectacular, with many muskegs, small lakes and ponds dotting the landscape to the south and west.

It was noon when I topped the divide, so I decided to eat my lunch before continuing on up the mountain. I sat down at the edge of a grove of cedars on the West Side of the pass where I could enjoy the view. As I ate my sandwich I speculated about the hunting prospects in the country before me. I had never gone down that side of the pass, but had often stood here savoring the mystery of unexplored terrain.

When I finished eating, I decided to alter my plan. I would go down the West Side and explore for an hour or so. I figured if I stayed on one drainage system it would be easy to follow it back up into the pass.

I moved slowly down to the northwest out into a large muskeg, through a timbered area, and into another muskeg. I crossed the creek, then started back up the other side toward the pass. By the time I got to the pass, the sky had become overcast with high, featureless clouds moving in from the south.

Because of the timber in the pass, I could not see down the drainage to the east. I walked east until I came to a creek that looked familiar, and started down it. After an appropriate time and distance, I came to the first pond and followed along its shore. I crossed the creek at the East End, then pushed through the bushes to the middle pond. I followed the east shore to the beaver dam, turned the corner out into the lower meadow and…

"What the heck?" No lake! My mind did a series of convulsive snap rolls. Panic and confusion washed through me like ice water. I stood there for a few moments, completely disoriented. Finally reason took over, as my mind pushed the panic away and started to function again.

"Okay. Think back. I went down the drainage to the west, then went back up it to the pass…I must have come down the wrong creek. I must be on the Skowl Arm side of the pass. This must be a drainage south of the one I came back up. All I have to do is follow this creek back to the pass, go over it to the east, and down into Herring Cove. "Simple," says my brain. Meanwhile, my irrational self is freaking out.

"Oh no, we're lost! We'll never get home! We'll wander here till we die of starvation! Bears will get us in the night! Ohhhhhhhhhh…" Swift kick in the mental pants.

"Okay, dumbo, take a break and let me figure this out. It's only two o'clock, got plenty of time before dark. Let's get going."

I go back through the sequence of lakes in reverse order to the pass. The sun is completely hidden by the high overcast. It's like being inside a pearl; no directional clues in the sky. I look up at the mountains on either side of the pass.

"Okay, stay between the mountains," I think, taking off down the hill.

As I go down, I'm soon in taller timber and can't see the mountains, but I come to another creek and follow it down into a gorge that I've never seen before.

"Damn, this is wrong, too!" I go back up the drainage. Soon I find another creek and follow it out into a meadow.

"Okay. There is a pond." I go down its shore, through the timber, then out into another muskeg. No pond.

"Crap! Now what?" I look at my watch; it's three-thirty, dark at five. I've got an hour and a half...

I decide to follow the creek down to salt water. I can spend the night on the beach in Smith Lagoon. It's drier and there will be driftwood for a fire. Also, I am familiar with that shore and can get my bearings in the morning. I know it's only about two and a half miles as the crow flies from Smith Lagoon to Herring Bay. I figure the others will be looking for me in the morning and I can fire a signal shot from the divide. If one of them answers, I'll know which way to go if I haven't figured it out by then.

I go on down the creek and come out on the beach in Smith Lagoon about a half-hour before dark. I gather enough driftwood to keep a fire going all night, then build a shelter out of poles and cedar boughs, with a moss bed. I get a fire burning in front of the lean-to and watch as the last remnants of daylight fade from the sky across the bay. I'm warm, safe, and dry. The panic is gone now and I chuckle to myself with the humor of the situation.

"Ole Dan'el Boner sure got himself in a pickle today, eh?"

As the night passes I smoke my pipe and gaze into the magic of the fire, lost in the dreamtime. I sleep some, curled in the moss, waking when the fire burns down, adding fuel. The pungent smoke and the odor of cedar boughs mixes with the moist night air to weave a magic spell that carries me through to morning.

As dawn creeps slowly into the sky, I awaken, chilled. The fire is only a few coals and my bones ache from the damp ground. I rake the coals together, add twigs and bark, blowing gently until flames spring into being.

The sky has cleared during the night, and as the stars fade, I stand, stretch, and then walk to the stream that trickles out of the woods near by. Bending down, I scoop the icy water to my mouth and drink. There are ducks on the bay and my stomach growls as the image of duck roasting on the fire forms in my mind. Realizing the futility of the vision, I walk back to the fire, light my pipe and wait for full daylight.

When it's light enough to travel in the forest, I scatter the remaining embers of the fire and pull down the shelter. I remove as much evidence of my presence as possible so the next person on the beach does not have to look at my leavings. A futile gesture, as this whole area is to be logged in a few years. I pick up my rifle and head back up the creek.

Working my way up the stream that I came down the night before, I soon top out on the pass. In the light of the new day, I easily see what happened. When I came up out of the first drainage on the West Side of the divide, I crossed over to the south into a parallel drainage instead of going east as I intended. When I came back up out of the second drainage, I did the same thing again: went down another south drainage, rather than the one to the east, where I wanted to go.

Forty-five minutes later, I walked out on the beach in Herring Bay. There were my friends, hunkered around a fire under a shelter much like the one I had built. Elden had gone home to tell everyone there what had happened so that they wouldn't think we were all lost, then returned in the morning with food. Dave and Karl had stayed the night in the shelter. There was a pot of boiled coffee on the fire and a box of sandwiches. We ate breakfast while I told my story, then headed for home, tired, but content with the world.

BLACK POWDER

One fall, I was in Ketchikan stocking up for winter. After everything on my list had been purchased and stowed on the boat, I still had a couple hundred dollars left. I decided I deserved a new toy to entertain myself during the long, winter months ahead. I just naturally drifted up the street to Jerry's Sporting Goods and cruised the shelves. Jerry had a whole section devoted to black powder guns and equipment, and I finally felt inclined to spend my toy money there.

I bought a .50 caliber Hawkin kit and all the necessary gear to make it shoot. It turned out to be a good choice; I got many hours of pleasure out of building the rifle and learning to shoot it. I didn't get to hunt with it that year, but really enjoyed casting my own bullets and fiddling around with different loading techniques. By spring, I could shoot a pretty good group out to about 75 yards, and felt confident to take it out for deer in the fall.

When October rolled around and fishing was over for the year, my mind turned to other pursuits, like deer hunting. I was anxious to see how the muzzleloader would perform. One calm, clear day I buzzed across Kasaan Bay to the foot of Mount Andrews, and anchored the skiff in a tiny cove, where the old trail to the mine starts.

It was an easy climb of about 1600 feet up an old trail that had been built during the 1920s. The trail climbed the mountain past the ruins of an old aerial tram that had hauled ore down to the bay, then it switched back and forth up through a grove of tall cedars to eventually come out in a muskeg, just below the top of the mountain.

At the upper end of the trail were the remains of a diamond drilling camp, left behind a few years before when a mining company from the Lower 48 had been re-exploring the old claims. Some of the small, plywood buildings were still useable, and we occasionally used them for a base camp to hunt the meadows on the mountaintop. Today, however, I would turn off the trail in the first muskeg, and hunt a basin to the south.

It was about a half mile around the bowl to the next peak south of Mt. Andrews. The whole area was muskeg, with clumps of yellow cedar and bull pine scattered here and there. It was ideal deer country at that time of year, and as I hunted slowly from meadow to meadow, I saw many tracks.

I would still-hunt along for a while, then stop where I could see out across an open area and blow the deer call. If nothing happened after ten or fifteen minutes, I would move to another spot and call again.

Eventually, I took a stand on a low ridge that was covered with stunted cedars and pines. On the end where I was standing, the trees were about as high as my head. The ridge extended off to my left for about two hundred feet and ended in a small muskeg. To my front was a big puddle of water about fifty feet long and twenty feet wide. Across the pond was a meadow that extended about fifty yards to a low, timbered hill. It was a perfect spot to make a call; the wind was right and I had a good view across the opening.

I gave a long, low bleat on the call, and had hardly finished when a big doe came charging down the hill in front of me. She came straight at me at a dead run, making a whistling, snorting sound. She stopped for a few seconds on the far side of the pond, then turned and ran as fast as she could go to my left. I didn't even have time to raise the rifle before she disappeared into the brush on the other end of the hump I was standing on. I couldn't see her, but I could hear her snorting and stamping her foot on the ground a few yards to my left.

The trees between us were open underneath; I had noticed this as I climbed up into position earlier. There was a space about three feet high that was completely open, except for the trunks of the small trees. I leaned down and looked under the lower limbs toward the deer. I could see all four legs from about the belly down. As I peered toward her, her head suddenly appeared, and she looked me right in the eye. She was gone in a flash. I saw her a couple times, bouncing away with her tail strait up and her ears laid back.

I had a hunch that she wouldn't go far, so I followed slowly, looking carefully for her. Sure enough, about a hundred yards down the hill I saw her standing, looking back at me.

I slipped behind a dead snag and tooted on the call. She snorted and circled out to my right. She was below me a little and I saw her several times heading toward my position. She didn't know exactly where I was, so she circled around to her back trail.

I lost track of her for a few moments, then heard a sound right on the other side of a bull pine bush just downhill from me, about ten yards away. I put the call in my mouth, then eared back the hammer on the Hawkin. I pointed the rifle at the edge of the tree she was hiding behind, and set the trigger. When I was ready, I gave a low call. She stepped out from behind the tree, right into my sights, and I pulled the trigger.

KA-BOOOM, the gun roared. When I recovered from the recoil, I was standing in a dense cloud of foul smelling smoke. I stepped sideways so I could see past the white cloud, figuring she would be lying there dead. When I was clear of the smoke, I saw her white flag bouncing off across the muskeg below me. I couldn't believe I had missed. She had only been about fifty feet away. I think I forgot how light the set trigger really was, and the gun fired before I expected. Anyway, I missed, and that was the last I saw of her.

I hunted my way back down to the boat and went home, disgusted with myself for missing such an easy shot. I got to thinking later; that old girl's ears must have been ringing for the rest of the day. I bet she will never come to a deer call again.

I finally got a nice little forked-horn with the gun a few weeks later. I had climbed up the side of Kasaan Mountain, watching for tracks. When I found a trail with fresh sign, I went up one more pitch to the next bench, then hunted along the side of the hill. The little buck must have heard me coming because when I saw him he was standing in his bed, looking at me. I managed to get a sight picture before the gun fired this time, and put a .50 caliber lead ball right through his noodle at about fifty yards.

I had the rifle for many years, but never did hunt with it again. I considered taking a bear with it, but never quite got around to it. I finally swapped it off for something else, and I have forgotten now what I got for it. I really came to admire those old timers who explored the west armed with these cranky old rifles. I guess it's like anything else, you do the best you can with what you have to work with.

CONTENDER

I woke up one morning in Port Alexander with a terrible urge to buy a new gun. I had about five hundred bucks that was burning a hole in my poke, and I had been agonizing over it for days. There was quite a list of practical things that I probably should spend it on, but I never could pass up the opportunity to indulge in my main interest. Guns.

I extracted myself from the sleeping bag and pulled on my boots and coat. It was pouring down rain as I climbed off the boat and headed for 4Js Gunshop and Tall Tale Emporium, but I hardly noticed. I just pulled up the collar of my raggedy, old wool coat and slogged on up the boardwalk. By the time I knocked on Jim's door I was pretty wet, and the old halibut jacket smelled like the ghosts of fish long dead. It didn't matter much at 4Js because the rest of the gang of ne'r do wells gathered there probably smelled just as bad as I did.

I banged on the door, then stuck my head in and yelled,

"Ahoy, anybody home?" Off in the direction of the kitchen I heard someone holler,

"Come in!"

I went in and pushed the door shut behind me. I slipped out of my wet boots and headed down the hall toward the sound of voices. The trail passes through Jim's gun room and the perfume of Hoppes #9 was almost more than I could stand, in my state of advanced vulnerability. I hurried on through into the kitchen, trying not to look at the rifles lined up in their racks.

Jim was standing at the kitchen table in front of the window with one foot up on a chair. The table was littered with beer cans and Jim looked somewhat worse for wear.

"Grab a cup; coffee's on the stove, help yourself. What's up, anyway?" he asked. I opened the cupboard and took a heavy, white porcelain mug off the shelf.

"Not much. Nice day, huh?" I said, pouring the cup full of foul black brew, then heading for the table. I pulled out a chair and sat down, nodding good morning to the other two taxpayers sitting there. I was doing my best to be cool and not let on that I was on a mission.

I barely managed to contain myself while the conversation worked its way through the events of last night's party, fish politics, and several other mundane topics. Finally, I couldn't stand it anymore.

"Hey Jim, where are the gun catalogs?" I asked, trying to sound nonchalant. "I want to look something up."

"You got that look in yer eye, Cap', what are you thinking about now?" he asked, grinning. He turned and picked up a stack of catalogs off the table behind him, then handed them to me with a twinkle in his eye.

Jim had a federal firearm license, and had been running 4Js Gunshop off his kitchen table for several years. I was probably his best customer, and he always had as much fun ordering something new for me as I had buying it.

"Oh…I've been thinking about trying a Thompson Center Contender in .44 magnum. I think it would make a great deer gun for hunting in the woods and along the edges of the muskegs," I answered, flipping through the pages of the first catalog.

"I don't know if I'd want to be walkin' around in bear country carryin' a single shot pistol with a scope on it," one of the other philosophers commented, taking his snoose can out of his pocket and packing his lower lip.

"Well, I'd carry my other .44 revolver too, for back up. I think it would be nice to have both hands free until you see something," I replied, finally finding the page with the Contenders on it. The discussion went back and forth while I was trying to figure out what I wanted. I finally decided on a fourteen-inch bull barrel and wrote the order numbers down on a scrap of paper and handed it over to Jim.

"Can you call it in today?" I asked, trying to keep the eagerness out of my voice.

"Sure, I'll do it right now. How do you want it shipped?" he asked, pulling the telephone closer, and starting to punch in numbers.

"The fastest way possible," I replied, grinning at him.

Jim is a master at using the phone. In a few minutes he was bantering away with some girl at the wholesale outlet in Anchorage, and soon had her promise to get the gun in the mail that morning. He finally hung up the phone and said to me, "She is going to ship it COD this morning; it should be here on Friday's mail plane."

"All right!" I said, hardly able to contain my excitement. I hung around for a while longer, spinning yarns with the gang around Jim's table. The coffee party finally broke up around ten, and we headed out to put the caffeine buzz to work on the day's chores.

The next three days were an agony of anticipation. Finally, Friday rolled around, and naturally the weather was terrible. The mail plane was on hold in Sitka for several hours until the weather finally cleared enough for the plane to make the dangerous flight down to Port Alexander.

After the plane finally made it in, Jim and I hung out at the post office while the mail was being sorted. Sure enough, the package had arrived. We wrote a check for the COD, then hurried to Jim's house to examine my new toy.

It was a beaut, all shiny black and smelling of gun oil. The afternoon gun shop patrons' forum was gathered to drink home brew and re-catch all the fish of the past season. Everybody had to handle the gun and work the action. We were like a bunch of kids with a new bike. Finally, after everybody had a feel, I slipped off home to mount the 1.5X Leupold scope. The pistol had a real nice heft and the balance seemed just right. I spent the afternoon monkeying around with it and savoring the joy of checking out a new toy.

Over the next few weeks I experimented with various loads and finally settled on a 240-grain cast bullet, lubricated with Teflon thread sealing tape. Since the gun is a single shot, I discovered that I could seat the bullet a lot farther out in the case than in the revolver. This made more space for powder and allowed the bullet to be driven at a higher velocity, without increasing chamber pressure.

As I worked with the pistol, I began to realize that it had the potential to be very accurate. I carefully lapped the bore with a series of fine and finer abrasives until it gleamed like crome inside. When I had the gun tuned to my satisfaction, I sorted reloading components.

I weighed all the new cases that I had until I could separate them into batches of approximately the same weight. I scratched a tiny mark in the nose area of the bullet mold to use to index the bullet in the case, then cast up a batch of 240-grain bullets. I weighed the run and discarded any that were over or under weight. The cases were also marked, as were the reloading dies. Each case was always run through the reloading dies with the marks aligned. During the bullet seating process, the mark on the bullet was indexed to the mark on the case, and both were lined up with the mark on the seating die. After the cartridge was finished, I weighed all of them, then batched them into groups of three.

On the range, I fired three shot groups at fifty yards. When each round was inserted into the breech, I lined the index marks on the case, with a mark on the end of the gun's chamber. After some tinkering with the scope and experimenting with different rest techniques, I was able to shoot half inch groups at fifty yards, and one day, one of the three shot groups measured less than .44 inches, center to center. When I first looked at it, I thought I had missed the target with two of the shots. On closer inspection, the hole was a triangle, just barely bigger than the diameter of a bullet. I was pleased, to say the least.

Next, I experimented with different carrying methods. I tried several homemade holsters, but they all seemed awkward. I finally settled on a sling made out of parachute cord. One end was a loop slipped over the barrel, and the other end was attached to a sling swivel stud on the bottom of the grip. The sling passed from the forearm of the gun, under the left arm, across my back, over my right shoulder, and onto the butt of the pistol. The length was adjusted so that when I pushed the pistol out in front of me, with both hands, the sling would come tight when the eye relief on the scope was just right. It was almost as steady as a shoulder stock, and really worked well if you could find a tree or something to lean against.

The sling also had a brass ring about a half-inch in diameter lashed to the cord, and a brass hook tied on about eighteen inches from the ring. When I was just carrying the gun, I could pull it around and up my back under my coat. I would snap the hook into the ring to take the slack out of the sling.

The gun was protected from the elements and out of the way. To shoot, I would unbutton my coat, unhook the hook from the ring, and the gun would drop down where I could reach it with my left hand. I would slip my left hand in under the sling on the fore stock, take the grip in my right hand, and push the gun out until the sling came tight.

It really worked well and the pistol was a pleasure to carry. It was easy to bring into action and out of the way when not needed. I also started using a walking stick that was the correct length to rest the gun on, and soon found that the whole system was deadly on deer.

It was the next fall before I actually went looking for a deer with the Contender. The day turned out to be a lot of work and left me a little disgusted with myself. It was a crisp fall morning and I got up early, excited with the prospect of trying out the new gun on the real thing. I climbed up into the muskeg north of town and sat on a hill over-looking a large, open area.

The sun was just rising over the mountains on Kuiu Island across the strait to the east, and the view was spectacular. The morning light colored the muskeg in warm browns and yellow-greens, and a light north wind made just enough ripple on the water of Chatham Strait to make it look like beaten gold.

I had been there about a half-hour, enjoying the view and savoring the warmth of the sun, when a tiny movement caught my eye. On a hillside, about four hundred yards to the east, a deer had walked out of a thicket of small cedars and was feeding around the edge of a muskeg pond. The wind was perfect for a stalk, so I slipped down the back of my hill and followed its base around to the south. I crossed a low area, careful to keep a small hill between the deer and myself. I eventually worked my way to the East Side of the hill the animal was on, and was able to approach to within about 75 yards, with the hill between us.

When I finally peeked over the crest of a bank, the deer was still feeding and oblivious to my presence. There was a low mound about twenty yards toward the deer, and I slowly crawled over to it, only moving when the deer was looking away. I made it to the hump and looked the critter over carefully. It was a small buck with two tiny spike horns about an inch long on both sides. It would be excellent eating and was small enough to be easy to carry home.

I took a steady rest over the top of the mound and put the crosshairs on the head. My confidence level wasn't very high that morning, so I decided against the headshot. I moved the crosshairs to just behind the front shoulder. If I had been using a rifle, I wouldn't have even considered a chest shot. It ruins the meat on the rib cage, and sometimes the animal will run off into the woods. A wounded deer is very hard to find in heavy timber. Contrary to my previous experience, I eared back the hammer and squeezed off the shot. The deer just hunched up, then turned and disappeared into the brush on the hillside. I stood up and reloaded the gun, mentally kicking myself for not taking the headshot.

I sat for a while on the mound, hoping the deer would only go into the edge of the brush and lie down. I knew the bullet had passed through the chest and the wound would soon be fatal. If I didn't spook it, would probably not go far.

I waited about fifteen minutes, then went over to where the deer had been standing when I shot. There was a wad of hair and quite a bit of blood on the ground. I followed the drops of blood into the brush until the spots disappeared.

The patch of small trees was only about a hundred yards wide and forty yards long. It was surrounded with muskeg on three sides. On the north end of the ridge, it was connected to another patch of bigger timber. I decided to go around the West Side and check the narrow neck of brush between this patch and the next one, to see if the deer had crossed there. If not, I would work my way through the trees from the north end, hoping to drive it out into the open, if it was still ambulatory.

There was no indication that the deer had crossed into the bigger trees, so I pushed my way along the ridge toward the south end. I found no blood and never heard a sound. When I came out of the brush, I decided to walk down the East Side of the hill and look around in the taller trees at the north end.

As I walked along, looking for sign, I saw the deer standing in the meadow, about thirty-five yards away. It was just standing there, calm as could be, looking at me. I raised the Contender and shot it through the head. "That's what I should have done the first time," I thought, as I walked up to where it lay.

The bullet had gone completely through the head. As I examined the carcass, I suddenly realized that there was no wound in the chest. I field-dressed it and found no evidence of a wound anywhere. It was obviously not the same deer. Often, these young deer will hang out together for two or three years after they are born.

When I was done cleaning out the body cavity, I propped it up on a hump to drain, then started circling, hoping to find the other one. I needed to leave the area as soon as possible, before the smell of blood attracted a bear. There were several roaming the area and I knew if one of them got a whiff of fresh blood, I would have company.

It didn't take long to find the other deer. It lay dead about a hundred yards to the east. It had joined its partner in the brush on the hill and they had both exited to the east while I was waiting for it to die. It had probably bled to death crossing the muskeg, and the other one was hanging around to see if it was going to get back up. I field-dressed it and pulled it over to the first one. It was going to be a hard morning's work getting both of them to the beach.

I made a pack out of one by toggling the front feet and pushing them through a slit in the hamstring tendon on the hindquarters. I toggled a front foot on the second carcass, so I would have a handle to drag it by. When they were ready, I put the first one on my back like a pack and grabbed the toggled front foot of the other one, and started for home.

I won't go into details, except to say that I was real glad to get to my skiff. I gave one of the deer to an elderly couple that were too old to hunt, and they were very happy to take it off my hands. So everything worked out okay in the end.

SNOW BUCKS

A rip-roaring storm had been pounding the coast of Southeast Alaska for several days. Fifty knot winds and torrential rains had kept me inside too long, and I was ready for some action. It was early December and we were still waiting for the first snow. The fall had been windy and wet and I hadn't been able to do much hunting.

Finally one night, I heard the wind switch to the west. It would be quiet for a while, then a big squall would swoop down off No Name Mountain and hammer the town. By morning, the ferocity of the gales had reduced and there were breaks in the clouds. The temperature dropped as the sky cleared and the rain turned to snow. When I got up, there was just enough of the white stuff to cover the ground.

I figured the deer were just as sick of the wet weather as I was and would probably be out wandering around this morning. I ate a quick, simple breakfast, strapped on the Contender handgun, and headed for the Ship Cove trail.

The trail goes across a low ridge, between the back lagoon in PA and Ship Cove in Port Conclusion. It's only about a ten-minute walk, and at the summit of the trail you are in open muskeg. The peninsula that forms the east shore of the harbor rises to the east, and No Name Mountain rises to the southwest. The pass between is mostly open country, and there are low ridges that give a good view of much of this area. The low saddle is a natural crossing between the two hills and deer use it frequently.

I anchored the skiff at the mouth of the trail and climbed up into the pass. When I arrived at the summit, I turned left toward the mountain, climbing up onto a low ridge that gave a good outlook. I sat there for a while watching the white, puffy clouds sailing by overhead, and enjoying the antics of two ravens that were performing aerobatics over Ship Cove.

It was getting colder as the sky cleared, so I didn't sit there long. When the cold started to creep into my clothes, I got up and walked on to the west. The country is cut by several gullies that drain north into Ship Cove. The ridges between these tiny valleys are covered with stunted yellow cedar and small bull pine trees. I drifted from ridge to ridge, checking for tracks and looking in the beds that are scattered along the ridges, but found no fresh sign.

There was a big, ominous-looking, snow cloud looming up over the top of the mountain, and it was starting to spit pelletized snow. I found three deer beds on the brow of a ridge, and settled into one of them to ride out the squall. I had good shelter under the branches of a cedar and a good view up the side of the mountain.

As the squall darkened the sky and the snow became heavier, I saw a deer come out of the timber up on the side of the mountain. It was hard to see it through the falling snow, but as it came down the hill I was able to keep it in sight. As it got closer, I could see that it's back was covered with a layer of snow, and more was accumulating as it came towards me.

In a few moments, it crossed the next ridge in front of me, then dropped down into the draw below my hideout. It trotted across the bottom of the draw right below me, then started up the hill toward where I was sitting in the deer bed with my back against a tree. It disappeared for a few moments, then climbed out onto the ridge about ten yards to my left.

There were two more beds between us and the little forked-horn buck walked right over into the one farthest from me. He gave himself a thorough shake from nose to tail and the snow off his back showered me where I was sitting. After shaking off the snow, he turned around three times and lay down with a grunt of relief. When he was comfortable, he started chewing his cud and looking around. He was so close I could smell him. I didn't dare move for fear of spooking him. So there we sat, about eight feet apart, enjoying the shelter of the trees and watching the snow fall.

We stayed that way for about five minutes, then suddenly he stood up, looked at me, snorted, and bounded off over the hill behind us. It was breezy; a current of air must have carried my scent to him. I got up carefully, took the handgun out from under my coat, and cocked it. I figured he would be standing a few yards away, waiting to see if anything moved.

I walked over to his bed and followed the tracks up to the top of the hill. There was a tiny hollow there and he was standing facing me about thirty yards away. I pushed the Contender out until the sling was tight, and found his head in the scope. When the crosshairs were on his forehead, I squeezed the trigger. He went down instantly, dead before he finished falling.

I reloaded the gun and walked up to where he lay. As I looked at him, with the red blood leaking out onto the new snow, I felt a moment of regret for shooting him. We had shared a special time together on that hill and I felt like I had killed a friend. I soon shook off the thought and began field-dressing him.

The bullet had passed through the brain and broken the neck as it exited. I was really beginning to like the Contender. It was easy to carry, accurate beyond need, and the load performed well if I did my part. I soon had the little buck home, the hide off, and heart steaks frying on the stove.

The next deer I got with the handgun was an accident. We had a big dump of snow overnight and it was still snowing hard the next morning. A strong weather system was passing inland to the south of us and we were just under the north edge of the clouds. The wind was strong out of the northeast, and as the cold, arctic air streamed into the low-pressure area, conditions were perfect for burying us in the white stuff.

About mid-morning, I decided to take a walk through the cedar grove on the low hill east of town. I didn't need meat, but just wanted some exercise, and to see where the deer were bedded. Also, I had a hunch the storm would last for several more days, and I figured I better get some exercise before the snow made it impossible.

I took the Contender along because it was easier to carry than a rifle; besides, I just plain liked carrying it. I left the house with the gun under my coat and my walking stick in hand. The coat was sewn up out of an old, green, and army blanket and had deer horn buttons. I must have looked pretty woodsy in the coat, my heavy wool pants and rubber boots.

I plowed across Back Bay and into the snowy woods. The snow was about fourteen inches deep and the trees were full of it. The woods had a sort of muffled feeling to them, and the occasional gust of wind in the top of the trees would send a great shower of snow sifting down through the branches. My coat was soon covered with it, and I was thankful for the hood that I had added to the coat.

I pushed my way up a slope, then scrambled over some half-buried, blown-down logs. I waded through thigh-deep drifts in a narrow pass through a rock bluff, then climbed a steep bank up onto the top of the low hill. This was the same spot where I had blundered onto the deer cashed by the bear two years before.

The hilltop runs north and south, with two short ridges that run east, perpendicular to the main hill. The tiny valley between these two ridges drains into a small muskeg in back of Judy's Cove. The timber is mostly Yellow Cedar with a few Western Hemlocks among them. Once you get up on top the underbrush isn't bad.

I plowed out into the more open area and stopped to catch my breath. It was hard work struggling through the soft snow and hard to tell where you were putting your feet. I walked a short distance along the main hill, and soon found a fresh bed with tracks leading off to the north. I realized that I had jumped the deer out of the bed and that it was right ahead of me somewhere. I knew that they seldom go far the first time and that it was probably standing just ahead, watching its back trail.

I pushed on slowly, stopping often to study the woods ahead. I came to the first side ridge, and the tracks skirted along the head of the small valley. In a moment I was at the brink of the drop-off into the cut and saw the deer standing right across from me on the other ridge.

We stood there for a few moments looking at each other. I decided to take a sight picture with the handgun just for practice, so I unbuttoned my coat and slowly removed the lens covers from the scope. I kneeled down in the snow and leaned my stick against a tree at an angle. It made a pretty steady rest, and I figured I could easily put a bullet through the deer's head if I wished. I already had meat hanging at home, so I decided not to shoot.

The Contender has a feature that allows you to put the hammer on half cock and dry-fire the gun without the hammer engaging the firing pin. In other words, you can dry-fire it with a round in the chamber without firing the cartridge. The trigger pull is the same, and the sear breaks just as it would from the full-cock position.

I put the hammer in half cock, put the crosshairs on the deer's head and squeezed off, just for practice. CLICK. The crosshairs stayed perfectly aligned, and the deer only flickered an ear at the sound. I eared the hammer back again and squeezed off another one. This time the deer turned and disappeared over the hill.

A flicker of motion caught my eye and I looked toward it. Slightly below and to the right of where the deer had been were two more standing on the hillside, looking up at me. I swung the gun over and put the crosshairs on the forehead of the nearest of the little spike bucks. I eared back the hammer and carefully pulled the trigger.

BANG! The gun fired. The deer tumbled into the bottom of the draw, stone dead. I was shocked. I must have pulled the hammer back all the way instead of just to the half-cock position. I felt regret; I had had no intention of killing it, and felt like a complete ass for playing games with another creature's life. I can barely justify killing them for food, and to shoot one by accident really made me feel disgusted with myself.

I reloaded the gun and pulled it back up under my coat. I picked up my stick and slid down to the deer. Once again, I had drilled it right in the forehead. Because I was shooting at an angle downward, the bullet had plowed a furrow in the skin on the rump after it exited the head, but no meat was ruined. I field-dressed it, then started the difficult journey home.

It went pretty fast. I was still mad at myself and used the energy of my anger to push through the deepening snow. I came out into Back Bay in front of the house that the schoolteacher and her husband were renting for the winter.

I decided to give them the meat. Jerreth was an Athabascan Indian whom I had met a few weeks before at a social gathering. He had lamented about the fresh moose meat he was missing out on by being away from his home on the Yukon River that winter. I figured he would appreciate some fresh meat.

I climbed up on the porch, shrugged the deer off my back, and knocked on the kitchen door. Jerreth opened it and looked down at the carcass lying in the snow.

"You want some meat?" I asked, when he looked up at me. His face broke into a big grin and some of the anger I felt at myself melted away.

"You sure?" he asked.

"Yeah, I shot it by accident. I already have one hanging and I sure don't need this one. It's yours if you want it," I replied. I helped him hang it in the shed, and he invited me in for a cup of tea. I told him the story of how I came to shoot the extra deer, and we spent an hour spinning hunting yarns and talking about guns. We became good friends over the coming months and I got to enjoy a lot of delicious, smoked Yukon River king salmon that winter that his mother sent down from Holy Cross. I forgave myself for killing the deer. It went to some people who really appreciated it and began a good friendship. I never did dry-fire at live animals again, though.

SUPERIOR

The old Superior bucked her way up Chatham Strait against a thirty-knot northeast wind on as fine a clear November afternoon, as you could want. As her sharp, black bow plunged into each trough, green water climbed over her bulwarks. It sluiced down alongside the deckhouse, then poured in a foamy cascade onto her main deck and out the scuppers. The big Caterpillar diesel rumbled beneath the deck, and the bellow from her exhaust stack changed its tone slightly each time the governor added the power necessary to shove her steadily forward against the white-capping seas.

The windshield wipers fought a losing battle with the spray coming over her bow. As I peered out the pilothouse windows, the water ahead looked like a white stairway to heaven descending from a brilliant blue sky. The snow-capped mountains of Baranof Island towered off the port side, and the Kuiu shore lay like a green fog on the eastern horizon. If you looked quickly, while the windows were clear between blasts of wind-blown spray, away off to the north you could just see the snowy tops of the mountains on the south end of Admiralty Island.

Suddenly, a great sea loomed ahead. The bow rose up over the top of the wave, then plunged down into the next trough. The pilothouse went dark inside as green water smashed against the windows and the crest of the wave crashed over onto the galley roof. The water carried away the stovepipe as it roared down onto the main deck.

The Superior shuddered and every timber groaned as she fought her way out of the trough, then up and over the next foamy crest. The second wave in the set was even bigger than the first, and another great dollop of water went over the pilothouse and onto the galley roof. There was a six-inch hole where the stovepipe had been. Enough water found its way down the stack to drown out the fire in the galley stove in an instant.

Big Jim was wedged behind the galley table, clutching a cup of coffee in one hand and a cigarette in the other, when the first wave landed on the cabin top. He heard the stovepipe go clattering across the back deck as the hot coffee slopped out of his cup, burning his hand. He hung on to the table as the boat staggered up the face of the second swell. When she hit the bottom of the next trough, the oven door slammed open, and the storage drawer under the stove slid out onto the galley deck, followed by a torrent of sooty water.

"Slow her down, Steve! We're taking water down the stove stack!" Jim yelled, as the boat lunged up toward the next crest.

Steve was already trying to get the autopilot disengaged and some revs off the engine when Big Jim hollered. The boat had been steering herself while Steve and Little Jim studied the chart, and the wave had caught us all by surprise.

"See what Pop is yelling about; I'm going to head into Big Port Walter and get out of this slop!" Steve shouted, as he yanked back on the throttle and wrestled the big, wooden wheel to port.

Little Jim and I lurched down the ladder into the galley as the boat turned her beam to the seas and began a long sickening roll to starboard. The galley was a disaster. The deck was covered with sooty water, and the pots and pans that had been stowed in the drawer under the stove had tumbled out onto the deck. She took another long roll to port, and as the boat rolled back to starboard, the cupboard doors all crashed open, spewing their contents out to join the mess on the deck.

All we could do was hang on and watch the slurry of soot, water, food, and cooking utensils slide across the deck and slam into the side of the cabin as she rolled back to port. On the next roll to starboard, she went over so far that I thought she would never recover.

When she finally stopped, there was a terrible grinding crash on deck outside the galley. I lurched through the mess to the galley door and looked out the porthole onto the back deck. The three hundred-pound steel hatchcover had slid off the main hatch combing and crashed against the bulwarks on the starboard side of the main deck. As I watched, the boat rolled back to port. The eight-by-ten-foot slab of steel plate and angle iron slid back across the deck and fetched up hard against the port rail with a ringing bang.

"Tell Steve to point her back into the swells and keep her from rolling while we try to get that hatchcover tied down!" I yelled to Big Jim. As I looked back out through the porthole, the hatchcover slid back to starboard, and I could see splinters fly as the corner of the steel slab bit into the bulwark timbers. I could feel Steve fighting her nose around to starboard, into the teeth of the seas, and when she stopped rolling Jimmy and I dived out the galley door. Little Jim grabbed a coil of line off a hook on the back of the cabin, and in a few minutes we had the hatchcover lashed down securely. Jim signaled to Steve, who was watching us out the back window of the pilothouse, that it was secured, and Steve turned her bow back towards the bay.

We were coming into the lee behind the north point of Big Port Walter, and when Steve turned her back abeam the swells, the roll wasn't quite so violent. We were soon in the bay and into calm water. Little Jim and I went back into the galley to help Pop swamp out the mess, and by the time we had the galley squared away, Steve was idling into the anchorage behind Clam Island. Jimmy went forward to help lower the anchor while his dad and I got the big oil range dried out and the fire going.

When the anchor was buried securely in the mud, Steve came through the galley on his way to inspect the damage that the hatchcover had done on the back deck.

"You guys havin' any fun yet?" he asked, grinning at our soot smeared faces.

"Any time now," Jim said as we followed him out the galley door.

On deck, Steve turned on the hydraulic crane. We hooked the cable to the hatchcover and lifted it back into place on the hatch combing. The steel cover had chewed some splinters of wood off the bulwarks on both sides. The damage wasn't that bad, considering the racket it had made, slamming back and forth across the deck as the boat rolled in the swells.

When the hatch was lashed in place, Steve made his way below into the engine room and shut down the big Cat diesel. We all stood around on deck for a few minutes, enjoying the serenity of the quiet cove and the relief that comes with turning off the engine after several hours in heavy seas.

It was getting on towards dinnertime, and there was a package of venison backstrap that had been thawing in the sink all day. We soon had spuds simmering and steaks frying in a big cast iron skillet on the oil range. When the food was ready we sat down at the galley table, and as we ate, we planned our strategy for the next day.

It felt good to be free of town. We had been trying to get out of the harbor for three days. The first "Blue Norther'" of the fall had hung on stubbornly and in our frustration we had decided to see if we could beat our way up Chatham Strait against it. Steve had a limited amount of time before he had to return home to Craig, and we were eager to start a hunt we had been planning for months.

We wanted to try some new bays north of our usual hunting grounds. They were remote enough that we figured few people hunted there. With the mating season just getting into gear, the old bucks would be feeling frisky and starting to cruise their territories, rounding up their girlfriends. Big Port Walter wasn't quite as far north as we had planned to go, but at least if the wind didn't lay down by morning, we could hunt there.

After dinner we told a few hunting stories over a couple drinks, then turned in early. Narrow and coffin-like as my bunk in the foc'sle was, it felt good. It seemed as if only a few moments passed before I could smell coffee boiling. I pulled on my clothes and climbed the ladder to the galley, poured a cup of coffee, and joined Jimmy and Steve on deck.

The wind had died away during the night and the Strait looked flat calm. The sky was clear and there was a light frost on deck, the first that fall.

"There he is; we thought you were going to sleep all day," Jim said, as I stepped through the galley door.

"Heck, it ain't hardly light yet; I can still see stars. Looks like a dandy of a day; you guys come up with a plan yet?" I asked.

"We were thinking of charging up the Strait a ways further while it's calm. Maybe go up to Red Bluff Bay or Nelson Cove," Steve said, sipping his coffee.

"Yeah, we could get breakfast over with on the way and get in a late morning hunt. With the rut on the bucks should be running any time of day," I answered.

"All right, I'll go fire up the machine," Steve said, flinging the dregs of his coffee overboard and stepping into the galley.

We followed him inside and found Pop at the table. He had a cup of coffee in one hand and a cigarette in the other.

"Well, you get something figured out?" he asked, as Jimmy and I refilled our cups.

"Yep, we're going to run up the beach to one of those new spots we were talking about the other day. The Strait is flat calm this morning, so we might as well make a few miles while we have breakfast," Little Jim answered, firing up a cigarette

"Sounds good to me," his dad answered, blowing on his coffee and taking a sip. About that time the engine roared to life and in a few minutes Steve came up the ladder from the engine room. He and Jimmy went forward to break out the anchor while Pop and I started breakfast. As we worked, we could hear the anchor chain clanking over the bow roller, and then the clunk of the anchor coming aboard. Steve shifted into forward, then throttled up the engine, and we were off for the day's adventures.

The Superior was soon pushing her way up Chatham Strait, her bow stem turning the calm water aside like a plow through fertile soil. Steve gradually increased the throttle as the engine warmed up, and she was soon making an honest twelve knots. The wake reflected the first light of dawn and looked like folded-gold foil as it rolled away astern. The sky to the east was turning yellow as the sun neared the horizon, and the night retreated to the west before its power.

When the food was ready, I went up to the pilothouse and relieved Steve at the wheel so he could eat. As the sun peaked over the mountains to the east, the Baranof shore turned gold-green in the morning light. The Strait looked like a silvery blue-green mirror, and the snow-capped peaks of Admiralty Island gleamed in the dawn light. There is something magical about the feeling of a sturdy vessel making good speed through calm water on a beautiful morning. The dawn light shining through the windows, the smell of varnished wood as it warmed in the sun, the taste of strong coffee on your tongue. "This is the life!" I thought, as I watched the miles roll by. "I wouldn't trade it for all the money you could pile on Baranof Island!"

The big Cat diesel rumbled below deck and the electric motor on the autopilot whined intermittently as it steered us flawlessly up the Strait. The others coming up the ladder from the galley awakened me from my reverie. Steve took back control of the boat, merely by being present, and we discussed a plan for the day.

We stepped off distances on the chart with dividers and figured running times to various bays. We finally decided try Nelson Cove; maybe spending several days there if the hunting was good. It was a bit of a run, but for some reason we were drawn there. The miles rolled by as we yarned in the wheelhouse and sipped coffee. The stories were of other hunts, rifles, boats, fishing, and dock life. By the time we turned left into Nelson Cove it was late morning.

As we idled into the north arm of the bay, Jimmy spotted a nice buck on the beach at the head of the inlet. By the time the echoes of the anchor chain rattling over the bow roller had died away, the deer had disappeared into the woods.

We decided that Steve and Big Jim would drop Jimmy and me in the south arm, then anchor the skiff at the head of the north arm. They would hunt that area while Little Jim and I worked our way back to the north along a bench that lay between the foot of the mountains and the west shore of the bay.

Little Jim and I climbed out of the skiff on a tiny, gravel beach and as his dad and Steve motored away, we loaded our rifles and pushed through the alders into the woods. There was a gully coming off the bench with a tiny creek trickling along its bottom. We followed it uphill until we came out in an open muskeg.

The meadow ran inland for about half a mile to the foot of the mountain. Right at the base of the hill we saw a small lake and decided to go over to it. The muskeg was crisscrossed with game trails, but all the deer tracks seemed to be several weeks old. In several places we saw the tracks of a huge buck that had been scouring the countryside for does.

We worked our way down to the lake, then up a small ridge at its north end. The tracks of the big buck were everywhere, but all were old. As we moved north, we stopped at several likely looking places and used the deer call, but nothing happened. The tracks became fresher as we proceeded to the north. We tried the call at each likely looking spot, but without success. After a while, as we sat watching a trail, we heard a shot echo from high up on the mountain at the head of the bay.

Eventually we came to a cut that went down to sea level at the head of the north arm. We could hear Steve and Big Jim talking down on the beach. Jimmy decided he would go down and cross over to the other side of the bay to have a look there. I felt inclined to go up the mountain to the west and try to call one out. The tracks were fresh there, and I figured there would be some immature bucks hanging around on the fringes of the old stag's territory.

I followed the cut up to its upper end, and came out on the edge of a meadow. There were fresh tracks on the trail coming out of the cut and I had a feeling this was the spot. I worked my way around the south edge of the small muskeg and climbed onto a mound with a bull pine growing out of its top. I had a good view of the tiny meadow as I sat at the base of the tree with my back against its trunk and.

Across the opening, about sixty yards away, was a small ridge covered with cedars that looked like a perfect bedding area. When I was comfortable, I put the deer call in my mouth and gave three shrill calls. I waited motionless and after about five minutes I repeated the call. As the sound died away, I heard a high-pitched whistling noise off to my left. I slipped the safety off the little Ruger No. 1 and gave one more low call. A flicker of movement caught my eye at the base of the hill where the sound had come from. Suddenly a great old stag of a buck took one step into the open and froze, looking right at me. I stayed totally motionless, my heart pounding with excitement.

I never have been a trophy hunter and usually pass up these old bucks, but this one was a once in a lifetime opportunity, although I don't even remember deciding to take him. After a few moments he looked over his right shoulder. As his gaze shifted away from me, I raised the little 7mm and put a 175-grain round-nose right through his neck at the base of the skull.

BOOM WOOM WOOM woom…the muzzle blast echoed off the surrounding hills. The buck had vanished, but I knew I had broken his neck. I levered the empty cartridge case out of the rifle and dropped it into the pocket of my coat. I slipped another shell out of my belt and slid it into the breech of the rifle. I slid the safety on and walked slowly toward the deer. He was stone dead, lying right where he had been standing when I fired the shot.

He was magnificent. The antlers were massive with three points on one side and four on the other, not counting the eye guards. I looked him over thoroughly, drinking in every detail of the big animal and the sights, sounds, and feelings of the moment. I felt a small sadness at having killed such a noble creature, but it soon passed. Man is a natural predator, whether we like to admit it or not. The satisfaction of using my wit and experience to take food from nature directly, without hiring someone else to do my killing for me, pleases some part of me.

After savoring the event for a while, I carefully field-dressed him. After removing the guts and cleaning my tools and myself, I grabbed an antler and dragged him across the muskeg towards the gully that led down to sea level. It was not an easy task. The carcass was heavy and the terrain was steep and brushy. It took about forty-five minutes of grunting, snorting, huffing, puffing, and cussing, but I finally towed the carcass out onto the gravel beach down in the cove and collapsed in exhaustion. I was covered with hair, blood, sticks, mud, and sweat. I could see Steve and Big Jim on the back deck of the boat, and after hollering several times, I finally got their attention. Steve climbed down into the skiff, fired up the outboard, and headed towards me.

"Boy that's a dandy; looks like the one I tracked up the mountain. Never did see him but the feet look like the tracks I was following," he said, climbing out of the skiff. It took both of us to wrestle the buck into the Lund skiff, and as we finished Jimmy walked out of the woods.

"That the biggest one you could find?" he asked, grinning.

"Naw, this was the little one. Didn't figure my gun was powerful enough, so I let the big one go," I said, trying to look serious. We climbed into the skiff and shoved off for the Superior. As we came alongside, Big Jim caught the bowline and tied it to a cleat while we scaled the side of the boat.

"All right, that must be the one we saw on the beach when we pulled in this morning; he's a beauty," Big Jim said as we climbed aboard.

"Yeah, he was up on that first bench just off the beach," I answered.

"That's funny, I hunted all through that area. Didn't see anything but a blue jay," Steve said.

"He came to the call; walked right out and looked me in the eye," I said.

"Well, I better start the engine so we can use the hoist to lift him aboard," Steve said, stepping into the galley and disappearing down the engine room hatch. Soon the exhaust stack belched black smoke and the big Caterpillar diesel grumbled to life.

Steve came out the galley door and went to the back of the deckhouse. Bolted on the wall was the row of hydraulic valves that controlled the articulated crane. I grabbed a scrap of line and climbed over the rail and down into the skiff. Steve swung the end of the crane out over the skiff and lowered the hook to me. I took a couple of hitches around a hind leg, then signaled Steve to haul away. The winch groaned as the deer rose up over the rail. I climbed back aboard as Steve rotated the winch to swing the carcass over onto the deck.

"Man that's a big deer. He must weigh a hundred thirty pounds or so," Jimmy said.

"I think it's the biggest one I ever got in these parts," I said.

"The horns are not quite as big as the one I shot at Big Port Walter two years ago, but the body is heavier, I think," Jimmy added. I turned on the deck hose to rinse out the body cavity. Jimmy and Steve went forward and hauled up the anchor, and in a few minutes we were steaming out of the bay.

We turned north up the strait and hunted one more spot that afternoon without success. We were just a few miles from Warm Springs Bay, so we decided to go there for the night. There was a dock to tie to, and the thought of a soak in the hot springs had a certain appeal. We pulled up to the dock just as the sun was disappearing behind the towering peaks to the west. Steve fried up heart and liver for dinner and when we finished eating, we headed for the hot tubs.

In those days the only year-round resident of Warm Springs Bay was an interesting character named Wally Sondenberg. He lived in an old clapboard building at the head of the pier. In the lower floor he had a small store, and his home was in the upper story. Across the boardwalk Wally had several hot tubs that were fed by a pipe from the hot springs. The place was kind of primitive, but the water was hot and a bath only cost two bucks.

I cooked my bones in the tub till I started to melt, then got out and walked on wobbly legs across to the store. Jimmy and his dad were already there, talking to Wally.

Wally was probably the worst gun nut I ever encountered. The walls of the store were covered with a variety of firearms. The walls of the stairwell leading to his home was covered with rifles and there were more in the apartment. He had about every kind of reloading tool imaginable and enough components to fight a war. He told us that he had used up 450 pounds of lead the first winter he lived there. He claimed that he had been some kind of Special Forces spook, and had worked for the CIA.

Over the years I have heard many stories about Wally. He has become kind of a legend in this area, and any good yarning session usually includes a Wally story or two. We talked guns with him for a while, bought a loaf of stale bread, then went back to the boat and hit the bunks.

In the morning we headed back south; Steve only had a few more days and we still wanted to hunt at Jerry's Harbor. It took most of the morning and early afternoon to make the run. Just before we made the turn into the anchorage, Jimmy was glassing the beach with the binoculars. He spotted a deer trapped in a grotto along a section of steep rocky beach.

"Look! There's a deer trapped in that crack in the cliff. It looks like it's hurt and can't climb out," he said, pointing out the side window of the pilothouse. Steve throttled the engine down to an idle and shifted into neutral.

"Let's run over in the skiff and check it out," he said.

"Yeah, okay," Jimmy said. The two of them ran down the steps to the galley and out on to the deck. The Lund skiff was on deck, so Steve turned on the crane and they hoisted the skiff over into the water. When it was floating alongside they piled in and headed for the beach. Big Jim and I watched from the wheelhouse as the drama unfolded.

Jimmy was driving the skiff and he nosed the bow into a sloping slab of rock at the mouth of the grotto. The deer was trying to climb the back wall of the crack but it was too steep, and the animal looked pretty well worn-out. When the bow of the boat touched the rock, Steve jumped ashore. As he approached the deer, it made one more futile attempt to climb the rock wall then seemed to give up. It stood with its head hanging down, accepting its fate as Steve slowly approached.

"Looks like a spike buck," Big Jim said to me as he peered through his binoculars.

"Can you tell if it is injured, or just tired? It must have swum ashore here and was either hurt or too tired to swim back out and go to a better spot to climb out," I said, shifting into reverse to keep the Superior off the rocks.

"I don't see any blood and all four legs seem to work. Some old buck probably drove him into the water and he swam here. Huh, Steve has grabbed hold of it and it looks like they're trying to load it into the skiff. Here, take a look," Jim said, handing me the binoculars.

I looked over toward the skiff just in time to see Steve, with the little buck in his arms, stumble into the skiff. Steve is a big man, over six feet tall and well over two hundred pounds. The combined weight of him and the deer almost swamped the skiff, but he managed to stay upright. I could see the deer thrashing around in Steve's arms, but he held on and avoided the flying hooves.

"Looks like they got it; they're heading back and Steve is holding onto the deer," I said, handing the glasses back to Jim.

The Superior was lying parallel to the beach, about a hundred feet out from the kelp line. I figured she would stay there long enough to get the skiff back aboard. Big Jim and I went on deck and when the skiff came alongside, Big Jim lowered the crane hook down to Jimmy. He hooked it in the loop of the sling, and his dad lifted the whole works aboard and lowered it on deck. Steve stepped out and put the little buck down on deck. It jumped straight up and when its feet hit the smooth deck they splayed out in four directions. The little buck just lay there, looking done in. Jimmy tied a line around its neck to keep it from trying to jump overboard.

"What the heck are you going to do with it?" Big Jim asked.

"I don't know; maybe I'll take it home to show to my kids, they would get a kick out of seeing it," Steve answered as we headed for the wheelhouse.

"Ought to just cut its throat and make meat out of it; after all, we are deer hunting," Jimmy said.

"Damn, you're really cruel. We just saved the poor thing's life and now you want to kill it," Steve said, grinning at Jim. Steve shoved the gearshift into forward and gradually throttled up to running speed.

An hour later we were picking our way into the narrow rocky entrance of Jerry's Harbor. It was getting on toward dark, so we decided not to hunt until morning. The anchor was soon down and set, and we went out to check on our guest. The deer was resting calmly on the back deck. Steve pumped some fresh water into a bowl and put it on the deck by the little buck. He backed away and the deer sniffed the water. It seemed to be just what the doctor ordered; it drank most of it.

"What the hell are you going to feed it?" Big Jim asked, lighting up a smoke.

"Good question, maybe we should turn it into venison," Steve said.

"Naw, I think we should turn it loose. It's in pretty poor condition, and we should be able to get all the meat we want in the morning," Jimmy said.

"Yeah, but how would we keep from shooting it by mistake?" I asked.

"You got any spray paint onboard? We could mark it," Jimmy suggested.

"Yeah, I think there is an old can of something in the engine room; I'll go look," Steve said. He disappeared inside and came back on deck in a few minutes, shaking a paint can.

"All I could find is a can of black, but I guess that will work. You guys hold him while I fix him up."

Jimmy and I grabbed hold of the deer and Steve sprayed an eighteen-inch bullseye on the side of the little buck. When he was finished, we turned it over and he did the same thing on the other side. We held on till the paint seemed fairly dry, then picked the deer up and threw it over the side into the water. The little buck made a beeline for the gravel beach on the south shore of the harbor. When it got to the beach, it walked out of the water and gave a mighty shake, then disappeared into the woods.

"That poor critter will never be the same again; he's had quite a day," Jimmy said.

"Yeah, the rest of the deer probably won't want any thing to do with him with that bullseye painted on him," Steve said, chuckling.

We went into the galley and stirred up dinner, then fell into the bunks, still cracking jokes about the target buck.

The morning brought clouds and snow. We were up before first light, having coffee and hot cakes. As the first gray light filtered into the galley, Jimmy went up into the wheelhouse to look around.

"Hey, there's a bunch of deer on the beach!" he yelled down the companionway. We trundled up the steps and looked out the windows. Sure enough, on the south beach was a small band of deer. In the middle of the bunch was one with a black target painted on its side!

HARLEY

Harley was a friend of Jim's who lived in Juneau. When they were teenagers, they had spent a lot of time together and had become life-long friends. I first met Harley in the early eighties. He worked for the city in Juneau, and each year he would take two weeks of vacation time in November to come down to PA to hunt deer with Jim. Harley's arrival was always a big event around 4Js Gunshop, and his presence usually livened up the place considerably. Harley would bring various goodies out from town, such as exotic food, boxes of fireworks, or some new gun for us to salver over.

At first glance Harley didn't look like your typical outdoorsman. He was skinny as a rail and wore wire-frame glasses with thick lenses that looked like they had been cut out of the bottom of a coke bottle. His appearance was deceiving however; he was a good hunter and a pretty good rifle shot. His eyesight wasn't very good, but he used a Red Dot scope, and if he could pick out the deer against the background, he would usually make a clean one shot kill.

One fall we took Jim's boat up to Port Lucy for our first hunt after Harley's arrival. It was a cool, damp day in early November. We planned to anchor the boat in the back of the inlet and try several hunts using Big Jim's Lund skiff to move around the bay.

We left town semi-early and got to Lucy about an hour after daylight. Jim was idling slowly up the middle of the narrow inlet while we discussed a plan for the day. About a mile inside the bay Jim spotted a big doe in a tiny cove along the south shore. We decided to shoot it for camp meat.

The plan was for Jim to nose the boat in close to the steep rocky point on the East Side of the cove. Harley would step off the bow and find a steady rest to shoot from. Somehow, in the excitement and confusion, Harley missed the fact that the deer was in the back of the cove. His distance vision wasn't that great and he hadn't spotted the doe yet. I guess he figured that he would be able to see it from the beach. Anyway, Jim idled slowly toward the rock point where he wanted Harley to get off, and Harley kneeled on the bow of the boat, trying to see the deer. All of a sudden, he raised his rifle, and aimed toward the shore along the left side of the bow. Jim was looking right past Harley from inside the wheelhouse, and when Harley raised the rifle, Jim looked at the spot where Harley was pointing the rifle. There was a tiny hollow in the rock wall, and just below the treeline were two fawns, looking right at us.

"DON'T SHOOT, IT'S A FAWN!" BLAMM! Harley fired just as Jim yelled. One of the fawns went down and the other one vanished into the woods.

"What are you doing, man? The doe is on the gravel beach, in the back of the cove. That was a fawn," Jim said out the wheelhouse window as he shifted into reverse to stop the boat. Harley stood there for a moment with a confused look on his face, then it finally soaked in what he had done. He was really bummed with himself and didn't enjoy the rest of the morning much. Of course we ribbed him mercilessly for the rest of his vacation, but Harley took it in stride. He got a nice three-point later in the day and that was balm on the wounds.

Another time the three of us ran up to Port Conclusion in the skiff to hunt a point that we knew an old buck had staked out for the rut. In some ancient geologic upheaval, a great landslide had deposited billions of tons of material in the bay at the foot of the mountain. It created a small peninsula that jutted out into the bay. The peninsula was heavily timbered with cedar and spruce and was superb deer cover.

Jim dropped Harley and me on a tiny gravel beach just north of the point, and we worked our way along a bench about a hundred feet above sea level, toward the peninsula. There was a well-used deer trail along the bench, and as we approached the base of the point, the sign increased.

We found the main trail coming down off the mountain, and I left Harley in a good ambush spot, then skirted around the peninsula to the east. The plan was for Harley to watch the trail, and I would go out on the point and blow the deer call. We figured I should be able to call a buck off the hill and it would pass right by Harley's stand.

I stopped in a grove of cedars that the main trail passed through out on the point. There were so many scrapes and horn rubbed trees that the air smelled of deer musk. I took out my call and gave several long bleats, then waited for action. After a few minutes I called again and almost immediately I heard Harley's rifle fire. There was only one shot, so I figured he had either made meat or missed. I decided to wait a while and see what developed.

I was standing with my right hand on the trunk of a small tree, with the rifle laying across my right arm pointing up the trail. I was looking off to my left, watching for movement and listening for any sound that would signal a deer's approach. I was just thinking about blowing the call again, when I turned and glanced to my right. Standing about twenty yards away was a dandy of a buck. He was looking right at me, and I could see his nose moving as he sniffed the air, trying to get my scent.

I had had the misfortune to break my right shoulder the winter before and it was still too sore to shoot from. I was shooting left-handed that year and it was really awkward. I had the butt of the rifle against my left shoulder and the forearm resting on my right wrist, with my right palm against the tree. The rifle was almost pointing at the deer, so all I had to do was swing it about a foot to the right and shoot.

I moved the muzzle and tried to get a sight picture. My brain was having a hard time trying to sort out the images and kept switching from one eye to the other. I finally got the left one looking down the sights and squeezed off a shot. I think I missed him by about a foot. I saw dirt fly to the right of his head, and by the time I recovered from the recoil he was gone.

I muttered something unprintable under my breath, reloaded the rifle, and went looking for Harley. I found him just finishing field-dressing a nice two-point. He said that both bucks had come down the trail together, and that the first one had gone by so fast he that couldn't get a shot at it. I had blown the call for the second time as the second one passed, and it had stopped to listen. He shot it through the head and heard me shoot a few minutes later. He figured I had probably gotten the other one, but unfortunately I had not. I had a good excuse though.

By the time we had Harley's buck down to the beach, we were glad that I had missed the other one. We managed to get tricked down into a creek bottom, and had to backtrack up the hill for some distance to find another route out of the timber. By the time Jim picked us up, we were pretty well hunted-out for the day.

One time we were hunting in Port Lucy out of Jim's skiff. Harley had dragged a deer down off the mountain to a tiny cove on the north side of the bay. When he had the deer down to the beach, he had followed along the shore to where we had anchored the skiff. When Jim and I came out of the woods, we all went to pick up Harley's deer. The tide was very high that day and when we arrived at the cove, Jimmy nosed the skiff into the beach just a few yards from the deer. Harley got out first to get the carcass, and I also stepped ashore to hold the bow while he dragged the deer to the boat.

There was a narrow shelf just above the tide line and a steep bank about fifteen feet high above that. Harley disappeared around a tree to get the deer and almost immediately he started to yell, "GIMME A GUN, GIMME A GUN, HURRY, HURRY, GIMME A GUN!"

Both of our rifles were in the boat, but I had my .44 under my heavy coat. I didn't know what the heck was going on; I could only see parts of Harley around the tree trunk that stood between us. My first thought was that a bear had been feeding on the carcass and was attacking Harley.

I tore at the zipper on my coat, trying frantically to get the big handgun out. Suddenly, Jim's rifle bellowed over my head and a big three-point buck came sliding down the bank and stopped at my feet. Harley came out from behind the tree, grinning from ear to ear.

He had looked up the bank when he got to the deer and saw the buck right above him looking down at him. When he yelled, Jim had looked up, saw the deer, grabbed his rifle, and shot it through the head.

Forever after, whenever hunting stories are being told around 4Js Gunshop and home brew emporium, the "Gimme-a-Gun" story usually gets told. It's always good for a couple laughs.

We had a lot of good hunts with Harley; unfortunately his last one ended in disaster. I was down in the Lower 48 that fall, so I wasn't with Jim and Harley for the last hunt.

Harley had brought his friend Dave down from Juneau that fall, and the two of them and Jim were hunting in Port Conclusion one afternoon. They had split up at the beach, and after while Jim and Dave heard Harley scream. They both knew that something terrible had happened to bring that kind of cry out of him, so they both went looking for him.

They found his hat, glasses, and rifle in a small muskeg not far off the beach. The rifle was jammed deeply into the ground, and they could see drag marks where a bear had dragged him off up the mountain. They followed for a way and found a trail of torn clothing and much blood. It was almost dark and they decided, wisely, to go to town to get help. It was obvious from the amount of blood that their friend was dead. They hurried home and called the state troopers. The police said they would be down at first light to organize a search.

Next morning the trooper arrived early and took several members of the community to search for Harley. As they tracked the bear up the mountain, they found more articles of his clothing and parts of the body. They finally found the bear chewing on the remains, about four hundred feet up the mountain. As they approached, the bear charged the search party and was killed at a range of a few feet. Luckily nobody else was hurt. It was a sad year for the whole town, and especially for Harley's family in Juneau.

There is much more of this story than I have chosen to tell here. I had the good fortune to not be there at the time, so all I have to go on is the many versions of the tale I have heard since. Almost everyone agrees that Harley had stopped to rest, and maybe blow his deer call at the edge of the muskeg. I have been to the spot where the bear jumped him. A few feet from where his rifle, hat, and glasses were found, there is a clump of bull pine brush. The brush was on a low mound and was flattened from many bears using it to ambush deer that passed below it.

Harley had stopped with his back to the bear and I doubt that he ever knew it was there, until it pounced on him. It was a poor salmon year, and the bears were forced to hunt deer to replace the fish they normally eat that time of year. I think the bear thought Harley was a deer.

KING OF THE HILL

It's mid-October. The weather has been rotten for weeks, until today. The wind switched to the west during the night and the rainsqualls have finally stopped. The forecast for tomorrow is for high pressure building in from the north, skies clear, and winds light and variable.

The old huntin' urge grows with the day. There is something about cool, clear, fall weather that brings out my predatory instincts. As I work through the day's chores, I find myself looking often at the mountains to the west. Images of muskeg edges, cedar ridges, and fresh horn rubs flash through my mind. I can almost smell the pungent odor of heather as the morning sun melts the night frost.

Scott stops by in the afternoon and we discuss local gossip, the government, gun control, and fish politics. We eventually get around to the subject that is really on our minds. DEER!

"Looks like huntin' weather to me," he says, as he twists up a cigarette out of a plastic bag of tobacco.

"Yeah, looks like," I reply, trying to look nonchalant.

"Marty and I are goin' out in the morning, you interested?" he asks, firing up the lumpy cigarette and looking at me with a mischievous twinkle in his eye.

"Does the bear crap in the woods?" I reply. We both grin, then bust out laughing.

"All right; you got any ideas where to go?" Scott asks.

"Well....I guess we could go up to Port Lucy, there are some interesting looking hillsides along the north side that I have always wanted to hunt. With this calm weather we should be able to leave the skiff about anywhere along there," I answer.

"Yeah okay, we can figure it out in the morning. I'll pick you guys up about daylight; it'll only take about forty-five minutes to run up there."

"Okay, I'll be ready."

Scott heads home and I get back to my projects on the boat.

The next morning dawns clear, calm, and cold. There is a light frost on the dock, but it promises to be one of those perfect days we are blessed with every so often, if you are tough, or dumb, enough to weather the rain in between.

I wake up when it starts to get light and start a fire in the wood stove. When it is crackling away and welcome warmth starts to fill the cabin, I put the coffee on to boil. While I wait for the coffee, I get my gear ready for the hunt. When the coffee boils, I throw together a quick breakfast and a peanut butter sandwich for lunch.

When everything is ready I pour a second cup of coffee and go outside to check out the morning. As I stand on the dock, looking around in the rich morning air, I hear Scott's forty-horse outboard fire up across the bay. I fling the dregs of my coffee in the water and move my gear out on the dock.

Scott idles up to the float and kills the engine. I tie off the bow line while he secures the stern to the bull rail.

"Mornin', nice day, huh?" he says.

"Yup, perfect," I reply, handing him my pack and rifle.

"You seen anything of Marty yet?" Scott asks, rolling a smoke.

"No, not yet," I answer, sitting down on the rail.

We soon see Marty coming down the pier. When he arrives, we exchange greetings and comments about the morning as we load his gear in the boat. When everything is arranged to Scott's satisfaction, Marty and I untie the lines and climb in, as Scott cranks up the Evenrude. He shifts into forward then throttles up, gradually bringing the big aluminum skiff up on step as we skim out of the harbor into Chatham Strait.

Chatham is glassy calm and the sun is peeking over the eastern horizon. The surface of the water is a sea of gold, accented with blues, blacks, purples, and greens. It shimmers like a sheet of undulating, multi-hued metal in the morning light.

We soon round Crow Island and turn north toward Port Lucy, grinning like madmen and shivering as the wind of our passage knifes through our clothes. We fly across Port Conclusion, then past Port Armstrong, Miner's Cove, and into Port Lucy. The mouth of the inlet points east and the rising sun paint the craggy mountain peaks red-gold as the light chases the night down their slopes. As we enter the bay, Scott throttles down to an idle and shifts the engine into neutral.

"Anybody got any ideas?" he asks as we drift in the middle of the inlet. We discuss several alternatives and finally decide to hunt the north side of the bay. There is a creek that comes out of a valley that has likely looking ridges on both sides. Marty decides to hunt the East Side of the creek and Scott and I will go up the other ridge.

Scott shifts the big outboard into forward gear and we skim the last quarter mile to a tiny cove just east of the creek mouth. Scott noses the skiff into a rock ledge and Marty hops off onto the shore. We wish him good hunting, then back out of the cove and head across the creek to a crescent of gravel beach that looks like a good spot to leave the skiff.

When the bow touches the gravel, Scott kills the engine and locks it in the raised position. We unload our equipment and I pack everything to the edge of the woods while Scott rigs the anchor. The tide will be coming in until the afternoon, so he lays out about fifteen feet of anchor line, then ties on the anchor. After wedging the hook in the ground, he ties on another long line, then uncoils it up the beach to the treeline. He ties the end to an alder limb and the boat is secure.

We shed a layer of clothes, which we will leave under a tree, shoulder our small daypacks, load the rifles and walk into the woods.

We are in a bowl-shaped hollow, like a bite out of the side of the mountain. Straight-ahead is a steep slope that curves around to the right and left. The walls of the bowl are broken by a cut that runs west to east like a crack in both sides of the basin.

Scott decides to go up the East Side of the bowl and work his way west along the ridge between the beach and the creek. I will go up the gully to the west and side-hill along just below the ridge top, the idea being that my movements would cause any deer that were bedded down in the timber to move up across the meadows on top of the ridge. Scott would be out in the open just above me and should see anything that crossed the ridge. I would also have a good chance for a shot as I moved slowly along through the bedding area.

As Scott disappears up the hill, I slip a cartridge into the chamber and click on the safety. I scramble up the west cut for about a hundred feet. It's a difficult climb; the gully is full of slippery flat stones and several tree trunks have fallen across it that are hard to climb over. After a few minutes of noisy scramble, I come out on a narrow shelf that runs parallel to the mountain in the direction I want to go.

The timber is a mixture of old growth spruce and hemlock, with underbrush of huckleberry bushes. The shelf ascends gradually until I'm about six hundred feet above sea level, then narrows and disappears into a talus slope that comes down a ravine. I cross the loose, wet stones, then pick my way carefully through a devil's club patch. After that is a nearly impenetrable tangle of blowdowns, which forces me up the hill about another hundred feet.

Above the fallen trees, I find a deer trail angling up through a grove of tall cedars. There is little underbrush for a while, but the hillside soon steepens and my route is blocked by more blowdowns. Beyond the downed trees is a deep ravine that is too steep to cross. To avoid the gorge, I am forced uphill and back to the east. When I finally find a place to cross, I'm at the edge of a small alpine meadow on top of the ridge. I cross the muskeg and find a vertical drop into a gorge. It is six or seven hundred feet down to the creek, and the view is spectacular. The mountains across the valley rise to nearly three thousand feet and their tops are dusted with new snow.

BOOOMMM....WOOOM....OOOOMMM..mmm. A gun shot echoes off the peaks across the valley. It seems to come from the east but I can't tell if it is Marty or Scott. I cut back and forth across the narrow ridge top several times, looking for sign that Scott has passed here. I find nothing but several sets of fresh deer tracks. To the west is a low bluff. I decide to climb up where I can see across the next muskeg and wait for Scott. It is too steep to go straight up, so I side-hill around to the left.

As I work my way around the low hill, the next meadow gradually comes into view. I stop beside the trunk of a dead pine to enjoy the view. The morning sun is painting the mountains across Port Lucy with beautiful yellows and greens and the water a thousand feet below looks like hammered gold.

As my eyes scan around the horizon, drinking in the dramatic view, they finally settle on the slope ahead. There is another small tree about 125 yards away. Lying under it, with the morning sun reflecting ochre-brown off his antlers, is a great old stag of a buck! He is a magnificent sight, lying there sunning himself and gazing serenely over his domain. His antlers are huge, and even at that distance I can see four points on each side.

My heart shifts into overdrive. I look around to see if there is anything I can rest the rifle on for a shot, but nothing will work. I'm standing in plain sight of him, and as I try to decide what to do, he turns and looks directly at me. We make eye contact and suddenly he is on his feet. He walks a few yards up the hill, then stops and looks at me again. My rifle is a Winchester Model 70, .338 magnum, with a William's peep sight. Even with a solid rest he is at the very edge of my range. I know that an off-hand shot is out of the question.

I raise the rifle and try a sight picture on his neck. The front bead covers the whole head and neck. I lower the rifle and look at him watching me intently. I decide to wait for Scott. He's carrying a Ruger Model 77, .300 mag with a scope; maybe he can get a shot.

Suddenly the deer turns and vanishes up the hill. I move carefully to the right around the small hill that is blocking my view. There is a well-used deer trail on the north side of the hill. I climb up to a small cedar tree and peer up across the muskeg toward the next hill.

The buck has stopped halfway up the bluff and is standing looking back down the hill to see if I am following. He's about 150 yards out now, and way out of range for my peep sight. The deer doesn't seem very spooked, so maybe he will stay around until Scott gets here with his scope.

As I watch from behind the small tree, I hear a grinding noise in back of me, like two stones under a boot. "All right, there's Scott, perfect timing," I think, turning to look back down the trail.

About twenty feet away, frozen in mid-stride, is another big buck. Our eyes lock for a few heartbeats…he makes one bound and vanishes into a gully, toward the cliff into the valley.

My heart hammers in my chest. I look back toward the other deer, but he has vanished also. I stand there stunned for a few moments, then chuckle to myself. What a morning! Two big bucks in a few minutes and I never fired a shot.

I walk back down the trail and follow the second deer's tracks into the small draw. They disappear at the edge of the cliff and I have no idea where he went.

I decide to eat my lunch and wait for Scott. I climb up on the small hill and savor the view as I munch my sandwich. Every time I flash back on the image of that buck frozen in mid-stride in the middle of the trail, I chuckle to myself again. I don't know which of us was more surprised.

I eventually realize that Scott isn't coming, so I head back down the mountain, following the narrow ridge. When I figure I'm above the basin, I cut down off the ridge toward the beach. The draw I travel down takes me onto the shelf above the cut I came up earlier. I rest for a while at the top of the last pitch, re-running the images of the morning's hunt.

After a while, I hear a sound above me and Scott appears dragging a doe. We work together to get it down the draw and out onto the beach. As we sit discussing the hunt, Marty comes around the point from the direction of the creek. He saw a couple deer but didn't get a shot.

Scott pulls the boat into the beach, coils the anchor line aboard, and then lays the heavy anchor on top of the line. We shrug into our heavy coats, load Scott's deer and our other equipment into the boat, then pile in and shove off.

"Look at that," Scott says pointing to the side of the boat. We look where he is pointing and see the words,"J. T. WAS HERE," written in blood with a fingertip on the inside of the hull. We look at each other for a moment, puzzled.

"John Thorington," Scott says laughing.

"He must have come by while we were up on the hill. I thought I heard a shot up the bay a while ago," Scott adds.

"Looks like he had a good hunt," Marty says.

Scott cranks up the Evenrude and we head for home. As the skiff skims across the flat surface of Chatham Strait, I replay once again the images of those two magnificent bucks. I'm glad I didn't shoot one of them. I hope they breed many does this fall and in the years to come. I have perfect memory trophies of both of them forever.

We have spent many a pleasant hour speculating about how to hunt the old one. The next year, Scott and I went back in September and hunted the whole ridge clear to the top of the mountain. We didn't find him but we saw his tracks! Maybe next year.

THE RUT

Sometime in late October a strange madness begins to creep insidiously along the muskeg edges and cedar ridges of Southeast Alaska. Something about the air is different after the first frost. Step outside on a clear, crisp morning and sniff the breeze. If there is the tiniest spark of the hunter in you, an irresistible itch will likely surface out of the dim recesses of your brain. It's been there for several weeks, simmering just beneath the surface of awareness, but today it leaps full blown into consciousness. Deer! It's time! Enough of this wood sawing, and lying around the house listening to the rain hammer on the roof, and the south wind rattling the windows. Enough salmon and halibut, it's time for some real meat. Heart, liver, backstrap, tenderloin steaks, a whole hindquarter slow-baked all day and friends over to enjoy it.

A similar madness comes over the deer about this time also. The bucks have been restless for the last few weeks, moving down off the alpine meadows as the frost line comes lower. The camaraderie they have enjoyed with their peers all summer has suddenly lost its savor, and the old mature males begin to drive the younger bucks out of their territories. Certain bushes also require shredding with antlers and rubbing with glands. Private mating areas begin to take shape along drainage boundaries, and each domain has a lord who patrols it regularly, freshening up the scrapes and driving out intruders.

Things really go crazy when the first doe comes into season. The perfume of pheromones permeates every hollow and glade, and all reason vanishes. The bucks run their trails from one scrape and horn rub to the next, with little thought of self-preservation and seldom bothering to feed.

As the does get closer to becoming fertile, they start hanging around the scrapes until the buck comes along and collects them. Each dominant buck has a small band of females that stay with him until they are bred, or some other Romeo steals them away. The whole process peaks in middle to late November and is usually finished by late December. The best hunting of the year occurs during those weeks.

The weather had cleared overnight after a particularly long wet spell. I had the hunting itch real bad and I was oiling my gun, trying to decide where to go first. An occasional rainsquall rattled through the rigging and the temperature was dropping. As I finished wiping down the rifle, I felt the boat tip as someone came aboard. I opened the door to find Marty shaking the raindrops off his cap.

"Morning cap, come on in. What's up?" I ask moving out of the way so he could come into the tiny cabin of my boat.

"Oh nothing much, I was just wondering if you were interested in taking a trip up the beach. Scott called this morning and wants to run up to Jerry's Cove and hunt for a few days," he answered, closing the door and sitting on the galley steps.

"Yeah, I'm up for it. I was just trying to think up a plan when you came aboard. When do you want to leave?"

"Well, we were thinking about running up this afternoon in my boat. Probably anchor in Jerry's, or Mist Cove, and hunt first thing in the morning," he answered.

"Okay, what time do you figure on taking off?" I asked, my mind already running through the list of things that I would need to do before leaving.

"I have to finish sawing up a log that I started on the other day, before the big rain, so it will probably be around one o'clock or so.

"Sounds good to me; I have a couple things to take care of too, but I'll be ready," I said.

"Okay, I'll see you after a while," Marty said, standing up to leave.

I spent the morning tidying up the boat and packing my gear for the trip. The westerly squalls had pretty much blown themselves out by noon, and the light north wind had dried off the dock. Marty's boat was tied about a hundred feet up the dock from mine. About 12:45, I started hauling my rigging up the float. While I was making the last trip, I heard Scott's outboard motor fire up across the bay. As I loaded my stuff on the deck of the Dorothy Ann, he pulled alongside and killed the engine.

"Hey, what's happenin'," Scott said, tying the stern line to a cleat.

"Not much, cap," I replied, grinning at him as I grabbed the bowline and tied it to the trolling pole amidships.

" 'Bout time the dang rain quit. I thought we never would get any hunting in this fall," Scott said handing me his backpack and gun case.

"Yeah, I was starting to grow moss on my back, it's been so wet. Oh well, keeps the tourists away," I said, chuckling. About that time Marty arrived pushing a wheelbarrow full of gear. Scott and I loaded it on the boat for him while he went below to start the engine. By the time we had his equipment on deck, the "Jimmy" diesel was coughing out white smoke and gagging its way reluctantly to life. In a few moments it settled into a business-like rumble down in the bowels of the boat.

"Guess we might as well untie and get going," Marty said, stepping down out of the pilothouse. Scott and I climbed over onto the dock and he untied the stern line while I got the bow. When all the lines were untied we shoved her away from the dock and jumped aboard. Marty shifted into forward and cracked the throttle.

As she idled toward the harbor entrance, we lowered the trolling poles and locked them down. There was still a swell running in the strait and we would probably need the stabilizers. The boat had no ice aboard, so she would be a bit rolly without them. When everything was ready, Marty throttled up and nosed out into Chatham Strait.

It was a beautiful afternoon, great puffy white clouds sailed overhead on the west wind, and shafts of sunlight shone down like giant spotlights. The tops of the mountains glistened with new snow and the air was cooling rapidly. The barometer had been rising all day; it looked like we were in for a few nice days. There was still a long ocean swell coming up from Cape Ommaney, but the waves got smaller as we steamed north.

The run to Jerry's Harbor from Port Alexander takes about three hours. As we rolled up the Strait, the sky gradually cleared and the seas diminished until the water was flat calm. Conversation was difficult in the pilothouse, so we spent most of the trip watching the scenery go by. I remembered other hunts as familiar hillsides drifted past and my eyes traced routes into areas that I had never hunted. Much of this country is inaccessible during the fall, due to the perpetual surge from the ocean swells. My mind is always studying the terrain, looking for ways into these un-hunted areas.

We eventually arrived at the entrance to the anchorage. Jerry's Harbor is a tiny lagoon in the middle of a small peninsula. The entrance is through a narrow opening in a rock wall and is tricky to pass through. There is a submerged rock in the middle of the channel and you really have to pay attention when entering. Once inside, you are in a well-protected little bay with good holding bottom and shelter from most winds.

Marty throttled down to an idle and let the speed bleed off as we approached the entrance. The boat glided through the kelp into the bay and we soon had the anchor down and set. Marty went below to shut the engine down and afterward we stood around on deck for a while, letting the echoes of the diesel die in our ears and enjoying the scenery.

The sun was already behind the mountains to the west, and the temperature was just above freezing. As the evening settled in, the cold drove us down to the galley and the cheery warmth of the oil stove. We cooked dinner and yarned around the table till about ten, then crawled into the bunks for the night. I had a hard time falling asleep, but eventually drifted off. Before I knew it, Marty was up putting the teakettle on the stove for coffee.

I rolled out of the bunk and mumbled "good morning," then climbed the ladder to the wheelhouse. The sky outside was clear and the stars were like icy points overhead. To the east I could see the very beginnings of dawn, and there was a half-inch of frost on the back deck. It was chilly in the pilothouse and after looking around for a few moments, I climbed back down the ladder into the galley. Scott was up and Marty was pouring coffee.

Over breakfast, we discussed a plan for the day. We decided to leave the big boat in Jerry's Harbor and run north a few miles in the skiff. There was a small sheltered cove to anchor in and some good muskegs to hunt.

It took about an hour to eat and get our gear ready. It would be a cold ride in the open skiff, so we bundled up in heavy coats and wool pants. Marty and I loaded our equipment in the skiff while Scott coaxed the outboard to life. When the motor would run without the choke, Marty and I untied the lines and shoved off. Scott soon had the big aluminum boat up on step, and we skimmed out of the harbor into Chatham Strait.

It was a beautiful clear morning. The sun was just starting to paint the tips of the mountains on Baranof Island a golden yellow, and their snowy peaks were reflected perfectly on the mirror-calm surface of the water. The cold wind of our passage cut through my coat, and tiny frost crystals blew off the bow into my face. The freezing wind brought tears to my eyes that felt like they were turning to ice on my cheeks. It was an exhilarating ride, but I was glad when Scott turned into the small lagoon where we intended to leave the boat.

We were all shivering as we unloaded our gear and anchored the boat, but the exertion of our efforts soon had the blood circulating through our veins again. We hung our heavy coats on the branches of a tree, shouldered our hunting packs, and loaded the rifles.

This was brown bear country, so we all carried our rifles fully loaded with a round in the chamber. We would be hunting in the hills around the drainage of a salmon-spawning stream, and the fish run was over for the year. The bears in the area had just enjoyed two months of gorging on salmon and would be hungry now that the fish were gone. Just before they den up for the winter they hunt deer, and so would be lurking along the same trails and bedding areas that we would hunt.

Normally, I would not consider carrying a rifle with a round in the chamber, but in heavy timber, the time it takes to chamber a round could be the difference between getting chewed or not. We were all carrying magnum rifles, which only hold three cartridges in the magazine. By loading the chamber the rifle holds four shells. I have heard of an enraged sow taking eight .338, 250-grain Nosler partition bullets at a range of about ten feet from two rifles. That is a total of about 30,000 foot-pounds of energy. I think I will risk carrying one up the spout!

Marty and I decided to go up the creek a short distance, then climb up through some meadows we could see above us. Scott would hunt the east edge of the same meadows, but would follow the contour of the hill around to the south. Marty and I would go up into a small pass to the west.

We worked our way along the creek on a well-used bear trail. There were remains of dead salmon along the path and several fresh bear tracks. I could feel the hair rise on the back of my neck as we pushed through the devil's club and huckleberry brush. After about ten minutes, we came to a feeder stream that trickled down a gully from the muskeg above. We scrambled up the tiny stream and soon came out on the lower edge of a big muskeg that looked as it continued up into the pass we had seen from the beach.

We stood for a while looking the area over thoroughly, then climbed slowly up the hill. All the trails that crossed the muskeg were filled with deer tracks, both fresh and old. We saw several horn rubs, and you could almost smell rutting buck in the air.

We climbed up about three hundred feet onto a bench with a few stunted trees along its edge. Marty blew his deer call a few times, but nothing appeared. When Marty was ready to move, I decided to stay put for a while. I had a feeling that this was a main crossing area. With Scott and Marty moving around in the timber above me, there was a good chance that some sneaky old buck would try to make an end run around them.

I got out on the very edge of the bench and found a place to hide behind a stunted bull pine. My perch gave me a panoramic view of a large open area with a major trail running across it. By the time I was settled in, Marty had disappeared into the pass two hundred feet up the mountain.

I stood quietly, leaning on the tree with my rifle across a branch, enjoying the view. I was about two hundred feet above sea level. To my right, about a hundred yards off, was a band of timber that came down off the northeast shoulder of the mountain. It went right down to the beach in the cove where we had left the skiff. In front of me, the hill fell steeply for about eighty feet, then flattened out into a gradual slope to the fringe of trees along the beach. It was about a hundred and fifty yards to the trees. On my left the muskeg sloped down into the small creek that we had climbed up from the main stream. There was about three hundred yards of open meadow in that direction. I could look out over the tops of the trees along the shore into Chatham Strait, and the view was spectacular. To the east I could see Kuiu Island, and to the north the snowy peaks on the south end of Admiralty Island were just visible. The rugged crags of

Baranof Island swept away to the northwest, shimmering in the morning light.

I stood admiring the scenery for a while. Suddenly a movement at the edge of the timber below and to my right caught my eye. A buck was standing at the treeline, looking back into the woods over his left shoulder. Before I could swing the rifle towards him, he started to run across the muskeg below me.

He was going flat out and I knew there was no chance of a clean shot. He passed right below me, about 75 yards out, but he was going so fast that I couldn't keep the crosshairs on him. He ran to the edge of the timber to my left and stopped to look back. He was standing right where Marty and I had come up the creek into the meadow. The range was a good three hundred yards, pretty far for a head or neck shot. I didn't want to shoot through the body and risk losing him in the thick timber.

I looked at him through the scope for a few seconds and finally couldn't resist the temptation; he was standing perfectly still and I had a fairly good rest. My .338 was sighted in for about 150 yards and would be somewhat low at three hundred. It's hard to judge range accurately that far away, and the bullet would be falling pretty fast at that range. I decided to hold just above the neck at the back of the head.

I wiggled around, and when the crosshairs settled just above the neck I squeezed off. The buck leaped into the timber and vanished. Obviously I had missed the neck bone. I opened the rifle and put the empty case in my pocket, then reloaded the chamber. When the gun was ready, I climbed down off the hill and walked over to the spot where the deer had been standing.

I found a few hairs but nothing else. I followed the tracks down to the main creek and found where he crossed. I searched for about 45 minutes but found no blood or any indication that the deer was injured. I went back and examined the hairs; they were all clipped neatly off with no blood or tissue attached to them. They looked like the hairs on the throat, so I figured the bullet must have passed just below the neck. I was shooting a 275-grain bullet, and it had lots of drop over that range.

I paced off the distance back to my ambush spot and got about 385 steps. It was difficult to measure accurately because much of it was uphill, but it must have been at least 350 yards. While I was climbing back up to the bench, I heard a rifle shot echo off the mountain above me. I couldn't tell if it was Marty or Scott, but somebody had made meat.

I sat down in front of the tree and took a sandwich out of my pack. I was somewhat disappointed in myself for trying the shot and it kind of took the enthusiasm out of the morning. As I ate, I thought about the buck and what a shame it would have been to wound him, then not be able to find him in the heavy brush. I vowed to not repeat the mistake again and after a while I put the incident behind me. The sun was shining in the meadow and it was hard to feel bad amidst such beauty.

I pulled my deer call out of my pocket and gave a couple bleating calls. I had been reluctant to use it earlier because of bears. The call is that of a fawn in distress, and if a bear hears it he will come to investigate. I had a good view around me and decided it was worth the risk.

After about ten minutes, I called again. As the echo faded into the mountain, a nice, fat, two-point buck came out of the woods right down the hill from me. He trotted toward me and stopped about sixty yards out. He stood there looking me right in the eye. I slowly raised the rifle and put the crosshairs on his forehead. When the sight settled into place, I squeezed off the shot. When I recovered from the recoil, the buck was lying where he had been standing with one hind leg kicking slightly as the last impulses faded away.

I reloaded the rifle and climbed down to the deer. The bullet had hit right where I had aimed, and I felt pleased for making an instant kill that wasted no meat. There is nothing worse than the ugly mess a high velocity bullet makes in the body cavity of an animal you intend to use for food.

I leaned the rifle against a handy bush and gutted the carcass as quickly as I could. This part always makes me nervous. You're up to your elbows in fresh blood, with North America's largest predator lurking in the area. It does add an element of danger to deer hunting, but I think I could get by just fine without that kind of excitement.

After I was finished, I cleaned up in a pool of icy water, then dragged the deer down to the beach. When I arrived at the skiff, Scott was already there pulling in the anchor.

"All right, that is a dandy," he said as I pulled the deer up on a log so it could drain.

"Yep, just what I was looking for," I replied.

"I heard a couple other shots; Marty must have seen something too," Scott said putting the anchor in the skiff, and laying the coil of line carefully on top of it.

"Well one of them was me missing a trophy. I tried a long shot but all I got was a few hairs; he was about 350 yards out and I shouldn't even have shot. Did you see anything?"

"Yeah, I went clear around into the next valley and found a nice three-point. I dragged him down to the beach in the next cove south of here and was just going to go get him, then come back and wait for you guys. You want to come with me or wait here?" Scott asked.

"I'll wait here and see if Marty needs a hand. I heard him shoot just before I got this one," I answered.

"Okay, I'll back in a few minutes," He said shoving the boat out and jumping in. He soon had the engine fired up and motored out of the cove, disappearing around the south point.

Marty walked out of the woods a few moments later, dragging a big doe by the foot.

We discussed the morning's hunt while we waited for Scott. We soon heard the skiff coming, and in a minute he glided up to the beach in front of us. We loaded the deer, put on our heavy coats, and shoved off. Half an hour later we were back aboard the Dorothy Ann, drinking coffee and eating lunch. Marty and I hung around the boat the rest of the afternoon, skinning out our deer and pulling the shrimp pot we had set the night before. Scott, being young and ambitious, climbed another mountain and shot another buck. He was pretty well worn-out by the time he got back to the boat, but a dinner of heart, liver, and fresh shrimp perked him back up. After dinner we had a few nips off the grog bottle and turned in satisfied with the day's hunt.

The next morning once again dawned clear and cold. The frost was so heavy that it looked like snow. It was too cold to ride in the skiff, so we decided to hunt the hills around Jerry's Harbor. We made a plan for the morning over breakfast, and decided to hunt the south side of the bay.

The harbor is on a peninsula that juts out into Chatham Strait. The southeast side of the bay is a low knob with some patches of open muskeg on top. There is a low muskeg pass between this hill and the mountain to the west. This has always been a productive hunt this time of year, and we were eager to get into the woods.

Scott wanted to hunt the mountain, hoping for another big buck. Marty decided to hunt the pass. He was having problems with his knee and didn't feel like climbing very far up the mountain. I already had all the meat I wanted, but felt like spending the morning in the woods. I decided to hike up over the top of the knob to the east. Scott and Marty should have gone with me. I saw six deer in the first hour.

Scott dropped me off on the beach at the bottom of the hill, then he and Marty skiffed across to the tiny beach where they would leave the boat. When they were gone, I loaded the rifle and went into the woods. It was a scramble up the steep slope to the top of the knob. I was out of breath and sweating when I got to the top, so I stopped for a while to catch my breath and cool down before heading out into the muskeg.

I was in a grove of stunted yellow cedar trees with little underbrush. There were several deer beds on the brow of the hill that had been used recently, and some of the trees had permanent scars in their trunks from old and new horn rubs. The cold morning air reeked of deer musk, and the main trail was well used. When I was breathing normally again, I walked slowly and quietly along the path to the muskeg. It wasn't far and I soon stepped out into the open.

The meadow was a fairyland of silver ice in the morning light. Every blade of grass and every tree was coated with elaborate crystals, some as much as an inch long. The sky was a kind of silver-gray high overcast, shot through with ribbons of pink. The sky colors were reflected in the frost, giving everything a slight pinkish hue. The meadow was about a hundred yards long and fifty wide, with a few small stunted pine trees scattered through it. As I stood admiring the view, a big doe crossed the south end of the muskeg at a fast walk. I walked halfway across the opening and stopped to see if I could see her standing in the edge of the timber.

As I stood there looking toward the end of the clearing, I heard a whistling snort. A huge old buck came out of the timber to my right and sauntered right up to me, walking with a strange, stiff-legged gait. He stopped about ten feet from me and made a low moaning sound deep in his throat. His eyes were wide open and I could see white all the way around the pupil. The hair on his face was matted with musk that was weeping from the glands in the front corners of the eyes, and I could smell it strongly from where I stood. He was so close I could see individual hairs on his body.

He kept swinging his head from side to side, rolling his eyes and moaning. I stood absolutely still, afraid that if I moved he might attack me. He was obviously highly agitated and looking for trouble. His rack was big, but not very well proportioned. There were three points on one side and two on the other. One eye guard was broken off and the other was only an inch long. I had no interest in shooting him. He was so full of hormones that it would be like eating an old mushy boot. Suddenly he gave another whistling snort and trotted off to the west. I don't think he ever knew I was there. He was so crazy with rut, if I would have moved he probably would have tried to mount me.

After he disappeared, I walked on across the meadow and through the thin band of trees into the next opening. This muskeg sloped down to my left, and there were two forked-horn bucks standing in the edge of the trees looking my way. They vanished in a moment, and as they bounced away, another one came out from behind a bush and followed them.

I crossed the clearing and hid in the bushes on a mound along the south edge. I could sit under the branches of a cedar with a screen of berry bushes in front of me. I was well hidden but had a good view of the muskeg in a 180 degree arc.

I let things settle down for a while, then gave a tweet on the deer call. I heard a snort about twenty feet to my left. Then I could hear sticks breaking and a rustling in the bushes. A small doe walked into view about ten feet to my left. She had me spotted but apparently couldn't get my scent. She trotted back and forth in front of me several times, snorting and rolling her eyes, then finally disappeared back into the woods. I called again and she came back to the edge of the trees to my left, but wouldn't come back out into the open. I could hear her snorting and thrashing around in the bushes, but she was too nervous to show herself again.

I finally started to get cold, so I stood up and stretched the kinks out of my joints. The muskeg rose to my left, so I walked on up to the top of the low hill and stood looking around for a few minutes.

This muskeg is always a hot spot during the rut. Some years ago I had shot a two-point on this knob, and as I was gutting it, a big three-point trotted up behind me and snorted. It almost scared me to death; there was fresh bear sign around and I thought it was a bear charging for sure. I swung around and the buck was standing twenty feet away looking me right in the eye. My rifle was out of reach, which was not very smart on my part. If it had been a bear, I would have been in trouble. The buck bounded off and I moved the gun over to where I was working.

I decided to go follow the tracks of the big buck I had seen earlier, and walked back to the other muskeg. I found his tracks in the frost and followed them west into the timber. He had gone to the top of a low ridge, then turned south for a couple hundred yards before dropping down the steep hill into the pass where Marty was hunting. About the time I started down the hill, I heard two shots down in the pass. I slid on down and stopped at the edge of the muskeg. I was on a narrow ridge that was the summit of the pass. Below me, to the south, there was a doe standing in the trail looking toward the west. As I watched, there was a shot and the deer fell in its tracks. A moment later Marty came out of a patch of trees on the hillside, and walked over to where it lay. I walked on down the trail to where he stood looking at the deer.

"Hey cap, good shot," I said.

"I missed it the first time, over on the other side of the hill. There were two of them; I got the first one and missed this one," he said leaning his rifle against a bush.

"Did you see the big buck that came this way a while ago?" I asked.

"No, just this doe and the little forked-horn that was with her," he answered.

"Huh, I saw him up on top about an hour and a half ago and tracked him down into the pass. He must have went north toward the harbor," I said.

Marty quickly field-dressed the deer while I stood watch. When he was finished, I helped him drag it up to the divide. When we got to the top, we left the deer and went west a couple hundred yards and got the other one. We dragged it to the main trail and started down to the beach with both deer. It was easy going; downhill all the way and mostly muskeg. The heavy frost that still coated the grass made the carcasses slide easily, and we were soon on the beach where the skiff was anchored.

Scott appeared shortly, and we pulled in the skiff and loaded the deer. When everything was aboard, we shoved off and idled over to the boat. We soon had the two deer hanging on the boom, and Scott and I helped Marty skin them. The task is easier when the carcass is still warm, and with the weather so cold and dry they would keep well.

When the hides were off, we cleaned up with the deck hose, then went inside for lunch. We shared the morning's adventures over venison sandwiches and homemade kelp pickles, washed down with coffee. Scott had seen only one deer, a nice buck, but wasn't able to get a shot. He still wanted one more deer, and Marty needed another also, so we decided to hunt the north side of the harbor that afternoon.

After lunch, we ran over to a gravel beach and anchored the skiff. None of us had ever hunted that side before, so we went into the woods and split up. We planned to meet at the top of the low ridge that formed the north side of the bay. Scott went up to the right, Marty went up the middle, and I went left toward the mountain.

After I split off from my partners, I climbed a narrow gorge with a creek in the bottom and eventually came out in a small muskeg just below the top of the hill. There was a low ridge to my left, and I could occasionally glimpse another muskeg through the narrow band of cedars growing on it.

About halfway along the ridge, it became so narrow that I could see clearly into the other meadow. I decided to go up to where I could watch both muskegs and take a stand for a while. I settled in behind a small cedar and started looking around. Right across from me, at the base of the mountain, there was a grove of small cedars. Two of them had bright yellow fresh horn rubs. They caught my eye immediately. When I looked at them, I could see a pretty little doe lying there contentedly chewing her cud, waiting for Romeo to come down the mountain and collect her.

I heard something behind me and looked around to see Marty coming across the muskeg. I signaled for him to be quiet, and when he came up to me I pointed out the princess across the meadow at the bottom of the hill. We watched her for a while, grinning at each other occasionally, and whispering about whether we should shoot her or not. Marty said she looked pretty small and decided to look for something a little bigger. The deer must have gotten our scent, because she leaped to her feet and took off up the hill.

We walked over to the horn rubs. There was a patch of bark about five inches wide and two feet long raked off both trees. You could see the gouges in the wood where the eye guards had grooved the tree trunks, and there was a pile of shredded bark at the base of each tree. The spot reeked with musk, and the trail leading up the mountain was torn up with fresh tracks.

We decided to follow the trail up the mountain. Once we were inside the bigger timber the underbrush thinned out and the forest floor was mossy with giant cedars growing in clumps of two or three along the hillside. The path angled up to the top of a ridge that fell off steeply into a gorge with a substantial creek in the bottom.

We followed the trail up the ridge until it branched, about 500 feet above sea level. Marty decided to follow the left branch that angled up through more cedars toward a bench higher up the mountain. I decided to follow the ridge top until I found a place to cross the gorge, then climb up the mountain on the other side of the creek.

After about three hundred feet, I came out in a tiny muskeg. It was torn up with deer tracks and I could smell buck again. I walked up to the middle of it and stopped under the branches of skinny spruce tree. It had started to spit wet snow, so I decided to stand under the tree and eat a peanut butter sandwich I had in my pack.

Standing under the tree eating my lunch, I could look across the creek and see up a steep muskeg slope. It was quite open with a few patches of small trees, and looked like good deer cover. I took out my call and gave a couple honks on it. Suddenly the whole hillside came alive with deer. They were in several bunches and I counted twelve of them, all does.

I called again just to see what they would do. It looked like the whole hillside was in motion! Suddenly I heard a loud snort down in the creek in front of me. There was a rustling in the bushes and a big two-point buck trotted out into the open, about twenty yards from where I stood.

He stopped for a moment, looking up and down the muskeg with jerky movements of his head. I tweeted on the call again and he came right up to me. He was so close I could have touched him with my rifle barrel. I stood there with my deer call in one hand, and a peanut butter sandwich in the other, looking him right in the eye.

"You better get the heck out of here, before I change my mind and shoot you for Scott," I said, taking a bite of my sandwich. He jumped about five feet sideways away from me, and gave a whistling snort through his nostrils, then he trotted over to the edge of the clearing.

He stood there for a few moments, snorting and shaking his head and rolling his eyes. All of a sudden he trotted back over to me. I thought he was going to charge, so I dropped the sandwich and swung the rifle off my back. When I moved, he turned and disappeared into the draw that he had come out of earlier. I could hear him rattling around down there for a few minutes, then things quieted down.

I picked up the rest of my sandwich, but it was pretty soggy. I pitched it into the bushes for the squirrels and put the wrapper in my pocket. It was snowing harder, so I decided to head back down to the beach.

About that time I heard a shot above and to the south of me. I worked my way on down the ridge and bumped into Scott, just above the muskeg where the first doe had been lying. He hadn't seen anything and was feeling pretty glum. We waited a while for Marty, and pretty soon he came down the trail dragging a fat forked-horn. We helped him get it down to the skiff and we were soon back on the boat. We were tired and wet, and the weather was changing, so we decided to steam for home. We had just enough time to make it before dark, so that's what we did.

It was a good hunt, we saw lots of deer, and got a good supply of meat. Scott grumbled good-naturedly that I saw all the deer, and didn't shoot any of them. I told him that when you walk around with murder in your heart, it spooks them.

It's funny how you can have spells when you can't find a deer, regardless of how hard you try. Other times you see so many you don't know which one to shoot. We tied up in PA about six-thirty. Scott and I helped Marty get his meat home and hung in the shed, then we helped Scott do the same. I lived on the dock, so mine would be safe where it was until morning.

I soon had a fire crackling in the wood stove on my boat. I kicked back in the glow of the kerosene lamp, to savor the memories of the last couple days while they were still fresh in my mind. I was living my dream; what more could a man ask!

PTARMIGAN MOUNTIAN

The August sun cooked the morning dampness out of our bones as we sat drinking coffee on the dock at Port Alexander. The commercial salmon-trolling season was closed for ten days, so we were enjoying sleeping in the mornings and loafing around the dock.

"Anybody heard a weather forecast?" Scott asked as he twisted up a hand-rolled cigarette out of a bag of loose tobacco.

"Northwest fifteen and more sunshine," I answered.

"We should go climb a mountain somewhere; shoot a deer," Scott said, with a rueful grin. Bodies shifted nervously on the bull rail. Coffee was sipped. Cigarettes lit. Deer season had been open for two weeks and we all had the itch. We had been looking longingly at the green alpine meadows as we ground out fifteen-hour days, trying to scratch out a living in a dying fishery. However, the thought of humping our over-forty bodies three thousand feet up some mountain and packing out a dead deer lost its appeal when faced with reality. The notion tended to sharpen the ache in lower backs, overstressed from years of packing firewood, shoveling ice out of fish holds, and carrying dead deer off mountainsides.

Scott's eyes speared me and I grunted noncommittally. I had turned fifty in January and wasn't sure I still had it in me. I was more inclined to do my hunting at the lower timberline a little later in the year.

"We could go up Ptarmigan Mountain in the back of Big Port Walter. It's muskeg most of the way; should be pretty easy going," Marty said, with obvious enthusiasm.

"Yeah, the guys at Little Port Walter have a rope up the cliff behind the old cannery. That's the worst part, then you just follow the ridge above Borodino Lake to the top of the mountain. I think it's about 3200 feet," Scott said, lighting the lumpy cigarette he had been rolling.

"I'd be into it," Marty said.

"How about you guys, ya up for it?" Scott said to Barry and Sonny.

"I'd go, but Heidi is flying in from Sitka tomorrow on the mail plane."

"What about you, cap?" Scott said looking at Sonny.

Sonny shifted uncomfortably and said, "I don't know. I'll think about it and let you know later. Sounds like a pretty ambitious hike for an old fart like me."

Scott and Marty both looked at me.

"Well why not. I'll go part way at least. When I get tired, I'll find a nice tree where I can sit in the shade and blow the deer call while you young sprouts work out your ya yas," I said with more enthusiasm than I was feeling.

"Heck, I could probably handle that," Sonny said chuckling.

"Maybe we should run up this afternoon. We could tie up at the hatchery in Little Port and run the skiff around to Big Port in the morning," Scott said.

"Yeah, okay, what time do you want to leave?" I asked.

"How about four o'clock, I've got a bunch of stuff to do at the house," Scott said.

"Sounds good to me, I've got some chores to take care of too. I'll see you guys around four," Marty said getting to his feet. We all went off to our boats to take care of business.

The day passed quickly and I had the boat squared away by early afternoon. About four, I rounded up my hunting gear and drifted up the dock to Scott's boat. As I loaded my pack and rifle aboard, Scott pulled up in his skiff and killed the engine. I laid my rigging on the hatchcover and helped him tie up. When the skiff was secured, he handed me his backpack and rifle case and climbed aboard.

"Well, ya ready?" he asked, grinning at me.

"Ready as I can get," I answered.

"Seen anything of Marty?" he asked.

"Not for a couple hours," I replied. "What about Sonny?"

"He called and canceled out. Said he had parts coming in on the plane tomorrow and wanted to get his engine fixed. I'll go fire up the engine," Scott said entering the wheelhouse and climbing down into the engine room. Marty showed up about that time, and as we loaded his equipment aboard, the exhaust stack belched black smoke and the engine roared to life.

Scott reappeared on deck. "Might as well untie; she can warm up while we idle out of the harbor."

When we had the lines off, we shoved out the stern. Scott backed and filled until the boat was clear of the dock. Marty and I pulled in the fenders and put away the tie up lines. Scott pointed her bow toward the harbor entrance and bumped the throttle up to a fast idle. We soon cleared the red buoy and turned left into Chatham Strait. Ten minutes later we were clear of Conclusion Point and headed north toward Port Walter.

Chatham Strait was calm and we made good time. The engine noise was too loud for much conversation, so I watched the scenery drift by and thought about the hunt. It had been several years since I had climbed up into the alpine, and I knew it was going to be a physical challenge.

We turned into Little Port Walter about six o'clock, and soon had the boat tied to the hatchery dock and steaks on the barbecue. The hatchery crew was just finishing dinner and several of them wandered down to the dock for a visit. Scott broke out a bottle of rum and a six-pack of coke, and a low-key party developed. Later in the evening Brad, the maintenance man from the hatchery, dropped by. When he heard our plan for the hunt, he said he would like to go along. We decided we would meet at the boat at five AM for coffee and hot cakes, then head for the back of Big Port when we were finished.

The party wound up about 9:30 and we crawled into the bunks after the last of the guests had left. I had a hard time getting to sleep but finally drifted off, and suddenly it was morning. Scott climbed up out of the foc'sle and cranked up the oil stove to heat coffee water.

"You want some hot cakes?" he asked, yawning and rubbing the sleep out of his eyes.

"Sounds good to me. I'm more interested in coffee at the moment, but I suppose we better stoke up with groceries before we go," I said, crawling out of my sleeping bag.

In a few minutes Marty climbed up into the wheelhouse, and not long after that Brad arrived. We ate quickly, washing the pancakes down with copious amounts of coffee.

"Well we better get going," Scott said, butting out his cigarette and putting his cup in the sink. We grunted in reluctant agreement and started rounding up our gear. A few minutes later we boarded the skiff and headed out for the days' adventures.

Little Port Walter is a narrow inlet situated in the mouth of a larger inlet called Big Port Walter. A long, low peninsula separates the two bays. The East end of the peninsula is broken into several small islands that end just inside the mouth of the larger bay. We passed between the end of the point and the first island into Big Port. The bay narrows about a mile back and becomes a deep channel between steep cliffs. The gut opens after about a half mile into a large lagoon, with towering mountains on three sides.

Ptarmigan Mountain's double peaks rise above the southwest corner of the lagoon. The south peak is about 3000 feet in elevation, and the north peak is about 3200 feet. As we glided into the lagoon, the tops of the mountains were hidden in cloud. There was a westerly flow of air, and as it passed over the tops of the mountains it formed a cloud. The sky to the east was mostly clear, but Baranof Island was shrouded in mist.

On the beach, in the southwest corner of the bay, are the ruins of an old fish processing plant. There is not much left of it, just some rotten piling, several iron boilers, and rusty steam engines. There is a low pass to the south above the ruins, with a waterfall tumbling a couple hundred feet down a steep cliff. Another stream comes from the west, out of a valley between Ptarmigan Mountain and the next mountain to the northwest. This is a fairly large stream, and has a run of dog salmon and humpies that spawn there in the fall. The mouths of these two creeks enter the bay just a few hundred yards from each other.

Scott throttled down the big Evenrude as we approached the mouth of the streams. The tide was high, so we decided to beach the boat on the grass between the two creeks. The trail went up the west stream for a way, then cut back to the falls and paralleled it up into the pass.

As we approached the beach, a bear that had been fishing in the west creek took off across the grassy tide flat in front of the old fish plant. As we anchored the skiff we could see much bear sign along the creek bank. It was going to be a spooky scramble through the thick underbrush along the creek. At least we knew where one of the bears was.

We soon had the boat secured and started up the trail. The woods reeked of dead fish and bear musk, as we pushed our way through the thick alders and devil's club. There were fish carcasses in the trail and piles of bear droppings. After about a hundred yards we came to an old wooden pipeline that paralleled the falls. This pipe was the siphon that brought water from the lake in the pass to the old fish plant. Much of the pipe had rotted away over the years, but some of it was still intact enough that we could walk on top of it.

We soon came to a nearly vertical cliff. The falls poured over it to the right and a few yards west of the falls there was a yellow, 3/4 inch rope that disappeared into the thick brush overhead. It looked to be about a hundred feet to the top of the cliff. It wasn't quite vertical but close enough. There were cedars growing out of the cliff in some places, and the rope was tied from tree to tree, kind of zigzagging back and forth up the hill. I was already tired and it looked like a brutal climb.

We slung our rifles over our backs and started up the rope. It was an exhausting struggle to say the least. The rifle was always in the way and the footing was poor. I was soon gasping for breath and sweating like a hog. My heart was hammering in my chest and I thought I would never make it. I could tell by the look of strain on the faces of the others that they were as miserable as I was, in spite of the fact that they were all about ten years younger than me.

The top of the cliff turned out to be farther than it looked from the bottom. After about 150 feet of struggling up the cliff, the rope suddenly ended in the bottom of a gully. The next stretch was barely climbable without the help of the rope, but after 75 more feet we pushed out into the edge of a big muskeg. We dropped our packs on a large flat rock and shed a layer of clothes.

After five minutes or so we caught our breath enough to look around. We were on a bench about four hundred feet above sea level. We could look out over the bay to the northeast and to the southeast was Borodino Lake. The lake lay in the bottom of a gorge with a narrow outlet. To the west, Ptarmigan Mountain rose in a series of benches until its twin peaks disappeared into the mist. The next pitch looked to be about three hundred feet and fairly steep. Much of the slope was muskeg, but there were many stunted cedars and bull pines growing in clumps here and there.

I sat on the rock contemplating the mountain. I felt totally exhausted and unable to go on. It had been several years since I had made a climb like this and the months on the water, with little leg and lung exercise, had taken its toll. The others were putting on their packs and discussing a route up the next hill. I decided to go up to the top of the next bench and spend the day hunting above the lake; the scenery was beautiful and the sun was peeking through the clouds to the southeast.

The next climb went easier than the first and when we finally came out on the second bench, I wasn't nearly as exhausted as I had been after climbing the rope. We rested for about five minutes, then pressed on.

It was like climbing a giant stairway, with each step three or four hundred feet. We would struggle upward, fighting our way through dense thickets of brush in steep gullies, or scrambling up grassy wet muskeg. Finally, after two hours of steady climbing, we came out on a rocky promontory that gave us a spectacular view down into the valley and out into Chatham Strait.

We studied the topo map and figured that we were at about 1500 feet elevation. Amazingly, I was feeling better. It was as I had gotten a second wind. My breathing was free and my legs felt strong and ready for more. We ate a candy bar and sipped from our water bottles, then went on up the next slope. We were above timberline now and the muskeg grass had given away to moss and wild flowers. Other than steep, it was pretty easy going.

The next bench was a bald rocky knob with a few stunted cedars on the south side. There was a sort of pass between the knob and the main mountain. We would have to give up about a hundred feet of elevation to cross it. To the south, the pass widened into a broad partially timbered slope that ended abruptly in a vertical drop to the lakeshore, several hundred feet below.

It looked like good deer country, so we decided to rest on the hill for a while and blow the deer call. Marty took out his call and gave a couple loud bleats. Two does came running up out of the trees to the south and climbed up into the pass. Marty tried several times to call them over, but they would only come part way, then run back to the other side of the pass. We had no intention of shooting them because doe season didn't open for another month. It was fun to see them and watch their response to the call.

We rested for about forty-five minutes, then crossed the pass. The next climb was up a steep rock slope that was easy climbing, in spite of the steepness of the grade. The ridge was narrowing and dropped off steeply on both sides. The view was really getting spectacular. We were high enough that some of the lesser mountaintops were below us. The clouds were thinning out and rising higher and only the very tips of Ptarmigan's twin peaks were hidden from view.

Just below the pass, between the two peaks, the ridge that we were climbing became almost horizontal for about a quarter mile. When we climbed out on top of this last bench before the top we decided to stop for lunch. We were pretty tired and needed a good rest and some food. We sprawled in a hollow under the branches of a gnarled old mountain hemlock that looked like a Bonsai tree in some Japanese garden.

It was an awesome place and we just sat quietly munching our sandwiches and looking at the scenery. The no-see-ums soon found us and called in the whitesox and black flies. The longer we sat there, the worse it got. Finally I couldn't stand the bugs any longer and got up and went on.

I climbed up a short slope and found myself in the mouth of a U-shaped valley with a long snow bank on the south side in the shadow of the smaller peak. In the bottom of the valley was a tiny lake. There was little vegetation in the valley, only some lichen on the rocks and some moss on the East end of the lake. I waited for the others to catch up and when they came along we decided to split up and hunt both mountaintops. We were only about two hundred feet below the summit of the south peak and four hundred feet below the higher one. The tip of the higher part was still sticking up into the clouds, but the lower one was clear.

Brad decided to go south around the lower mountain; Scot and Marty would climb the higher one. I was curious about the pass between the two summits, so I walked along the south shore of the lake and climbed up a talus slope of about 100 feet into the pass. There was quite a lot of deer sign and bear sign, which amazed me, considering the lack of vegetation.

When I finally topped out in the pass, the view was breath taking! I was on the spine of Baranof Island. All the water from this point on flowed into the ocean on the West side of the island, rather than into the strait. To the south, the back of the mountains looked as they had been split by some giant upheaval. It dropped off, straight down, for about a thousand feet. Below me was a basin with a small green lake in the bottom. The out let of the lake was a gorge that disappeared around to the northwest. I could hear the roar of a falls and see mist coming up out of the cut.

I climbed down to a tiny ledge about fifty feet below the summit of the pass and sat with my back against a rock. It was warm there and I had a good view of the basin below. I dug my binoculars out of the pack and scanned the valley. I was looking along the south shore of the lake. Suddenly a deer came out of some bushes and slid down a bank to the lake. When he got to the water's edge, he drank for a while, then walked toward me along the shore.

There was a large flat area directly below my perch with a creek running across it. The only vegetation was a few sparse clumps of grass and some moss along the stream. The deer came around the end of the pond, then trotted purposefully across the gravel flat to the creek. It splashed across the stream and went to a brown spot that I suddenly realized was another deer. It was lying down in the gravel and the first deer walked up to it and pawed at it several times with a front foot. The second deer leaped to its feet and they both reared up on their hind legs and pawed each other for a few seconds.

When they were finished with this strange ritual they both crossed the creek and lay down among some large flat rocks. As I studied the gravel flat below me, I discovered several more deer lying in various locations along the creek. They were too far away to tell if they had antlers, and too far down the wrong side of the mountain to stalk.

After watching them for a while, I climbed back into the pass. I could see Marty and Scott up on the side of the main peak. They were slowly working their way down into the pass. I waited for them and we went down onto the ledge and watched the deer for a while. It was well into the afternoon, so we decided we better go find Brad and head back down the mountain.

We climbed back into the pass and down into the valley. Brad came down off the East side of the lower peak and said that he had killed a buck on the other side and needed help getting it to the ridge. We followed him across the ridge just below the summit, then about three hundred feet down the south side of the mountain. He had shot the buck just below the top and it had rolled down and hung up on a ledge. He had field-dressed it and tried to drag it back up the mountain, but found it impossible.

We boned out the carcass and divided up the load four ways. We each wound up with about twenty pounds of meat. It doesn't sound like much, but it was a grunt packing it up and over that hill. We ribbed Brad mercilessly for shooting it on the wrong side of the mountain, but he took it good-naturedly.

The trip back down the mountain went pretty fast. Our legs were really tired and getting wobbly, but in spite of some spectacular pratt falls, we made it down without mishap. We got to the skiff at about five-thirty; wet, tired, hungry, and full of satisfaction for our day's work. We saw another bear fishing in the creek, but he took off when he saw us. The tide had gone out and came back in while we were on the mountain, so the skiff was floating serenely in the mouth of the creek. We soon had our gear aboard and were skimming across the calm water toward Little Port.

Brad's wife, Jen, invited us for dinner, so we changed clothes on the boat and walked up the gravel path to their house. We had a pleasant evening, drinking Brad's home brew beer and enjoying the excellent dinner Jen had fixed for us. We stayed till about ten-thirty then went back to the boat and fell into an exhausted slumber. In the morning we headed back to PA. There were no trophy racks to brag about, but we had the memories of a great adventure to share among others and ourselves if they were interested enough to listen.

WILDCAT

One spring I got a chance to buy a 03-A3 Springfield army rifle from a fella who was heading south for greener pastures. I had been hankering to try a 35 Whelen, and at that time there were no factory rifles chambered in that caliber available. Deer hunting in brown bear country is always kind of exciting, and a person tends to gravitate toward bigger guns. At the time, I was hunting with a Ruger # 1 in 7mm Mauser. This is a great deer cartridge, but that little 175-grain bullet looks pretty puny when you happen upon a twelve-inch wide bear track while sneaking up your favorite cedar ridge.

I had been reading such worthy wise men as Elmer Keith and Jack O'Conner, and tended to agree with them that something with a little bigger bullet was in order. Both gentlemen spoke highly of the necked up '06, and after much agonizing, I decided that was what I wanted. The old Springfield sort of serendipitously appeared about that time, so I bought it.

I found an address for a gunsmith in Omack, Washington who did re-boring and chambering. We exchanged a series of letters and he eventually agreed to do the work for me. I stripped the rifle down to just the barreled action and mailed it to him in a length of PVC pipe.

It seemed to take forever before it showed back up at the post office, but it eventually did. The new rifling was crisp and clean and I could hardly contain myself. During the summer I had ordered a semi-inletted stock blank from Rienhard Fajen and the tools I would need to finish it. It took about three weeks to inlet the stock and finish the outside. However the finished product was worth the effort. I did it classical style, with a cheek piece but no Monty Carlo in the but stock. The finish was several thin coats of varnish thinned with tongue oil, and sanded lightly between coats. I wanted a good sealer but no coating of varnish on the outside of the wood. I finished by rubbing linseed oil on with my hand over a period of several days, then letting it dry for another week. It came out very nice and I was pleased with the results.

The receiver was already drilled and tapped for a Weaver mount, and I had an old Weaver K1 scope with a blued steel tube, instead of painted aluminum. It nicely matched the bluing on the barrel and action and gave the rifle a classic 1940's look that I really liked. It was nice, but not so fancy that it couldn't be used. I didn't build it for show. I built it to use!

At that time, Hornady was making a 250-grain round-nose bullet in .358 diameter, and I had ordered several boxes of them along with a set of reloading dies from Brownells. I really had a good time working up a load for that rifle. The cases were easy to form out of 30-06 brass, and the rifle didn't seem to be particular. It was very stable and I soon had it shooting inch and a half triangles at 100 yards. With a higher-power scope, it would have shot a tighter group. For short range hunting in thick timber and muskeg, the 0-magnification scope was just fine. The field of view was enormous compared to a magnifying scope. I sighted it in to hit about an inch high at 100 yards and called it finished.

It was early October by the time the rifle was ready, and the muskegs had already turned brown. There was new snow on the mountains to the west, and I figured there should be a deer or two hanging out in the muskeg northeast of town. The first nice day after the rifle was ready, I walked over to Judy's Cove just as it was getting light. I climbed up through the timber to the small plateau above town.

There is a kind of rim that runs east to west along the south edge of the muskeg, and the land slopes gradually down to the northeast. It is a great place to sit and watch for deer that time of year. When I got to the top of the rim, I found a place where I could stand under the limbs of a stunted pine and rest the rifle over a branch. I was well hidden and had a good view out across the muskeg.

When I was settled in I took out my deer call and gave a series of bleats. It was a perfect morning; the sun was just coming up to my right and the morning rays painted the meadow in a spectacular orange-yellow glow. There was a light northeast wind blowing out in Chatham Strait, and the water was an icy blue in contrast to the warm hues of the hilltop.

I tweeted on the call a few more times and waited, scanning the muskeg looking for movement. There was a flock of tiny, gray-brown birds feeding in a bush behind me, and as I waited I could hear them discussing their morning meal. Suddenly I heard a whirring noise and a high pitched squeak. I turned and looked toward the bush just in time to see a small hawk flare out and snatch one of the tiny birds in his talons. Clutching its prey, it flapped away toward the hill across the muskeg. The incident happened about ten feet from my nose. It was quite a sight to see that hawk, with his wings spread, reach out at just the right instant and pluck the small bird off the branch.

As I watched the hawk disappear into the distance, I caught another movement off to my left. A big, mature doe had appeared about three hundred yards around the rim from my hideout. She stopped for a moment, then trotted out into the muskeg, angling across from left to right. She ran across a small gully and up the other side. I gave a loud bleat on the call and she stopped about 250 yards out and looked my way.

I looked at her through the scope and realized that she was probably too far away for a sure kill. I did some calculations in my head and figured that if I held just above the neck, I would either break the neck or shoot under. I decided to try it. I usually don't take long shots, but I was curious about the new rifle. When the crosshairs looked right, I squeezed off the shot.

BOOMM…. WOCK. The bullet seemed to take a long time to get there but it sounded like it hit pretty solidly. I bolted another cartridge into the chamber and waited to see if she would get up, but she never moved.

I opened the rifle and reloaded the magazine. I knew better, than to try packing out a deer in bear country with the rifle unloaded. I paced off the distance to the carcass and came up with 275 paces. This distance was stepped off down across a shallow gully and up the other side, so the actual distance was probably around 240-260 yards. It is hard to measure distance accurately in that kind of terrain.

In any case, it was the longest shot I had ever made. The bullet broke the spine just below the head, pretty much where I had been aiming. I was tickled pink. I had made a good clean kill at long range, with a rifle I had built myself and a load I had developed for it. Very satisfying. Unfortunately the next episode didn't go quite so well.

Some weeks later I was cruising the beach in Port Conclusion, looking for a couple firewood logs to tow home and hoping to see a deer. The snowline was pretty far down the mountain and the rut was in full swing. I figured my chances of getting some meat were pretty good. I decided to run across to the north side of the bay, just south of Port Armstrong, and cruise the beach back south, looking for a log. There was a point that stuck out into the bay about halfway around, and I thought I might get out and take the rifle for a walk when I got there.

In the northwest corner of Conclusion there is a shallow bight called John's Bay. There is a big creek running into it's south side that has deposited a gravel bar along the back of the bay. It was low tide and the gravel bar at the mouth of the creek came way out into the middle of the bay. When I came around the north point, into John's Bay, I could see a big old buck standing on the bank of the creek where it spilled into the bay.

There was no place I could get ashore within range, so I decided to see how close I could get in the skiff. I idled in toward the creek mouth with the little Evenrude barely ticking over. The deer was licking salt water off the stones in the mouth of the stream and seemed oblivious to my approach.

When I was about fifty yards from him, I killed the engine. The buck's head came up and he looked right at me. He stood for a moment, then turned around, walked about ten feet, then stopped and looked over his shoulder.

I had raised the rifle as he walked away and had my foot up on the middle seat with my left elbow resting on it. It was fairly steady, but I decided not to shoot for the head or neck. He was pretty much broadside, so I put the crosshairs just behind the shoulder and fired.

As luck would have it, the deer took a step just as I pulled the trigger. The big round-nose bullet took him right in the cheek of the ass. It knocked him down, but he got right up and took off for the woods, with the broken leg flopping along behind.

"Damnit! Why didn't you go for the headshot? Now look what you've done," I thought to myself as I bolted in another cartridge. I didn't even try another shot; I knew I couldn't make a killing shot out of the skiff with the deer running. I marked the spot where he went into the woods, started the outboard, and motored to the beach. I took my time anchoring the skiff out, then reloaded the rifle and walked slowly over to the steep bank he had climbed to get into the woods.

The creek had a good run of dog salmon and pinks and the bank was littered with remains of dead fish. There were piles of bear dung and I was not relishing the idea of following the deer into the woods. There was no way, though, that I was going to go away and leave that animal to suffer. I had wounded him and it was my responsibility to go find him.

There was a lot of blood at the mouth of the trail, and I could see where he had fallen down and struggled back to his feet. I followed the drops of blood for about twenty yards just inside the treeline, then the trail passed around the roots of a big tree that had fallen into the creek. The trail went around the root mass, and I found the buck lying in the hole that the roots had left when the tree fell. He was mostly dead, but was still able to raise his head and look at me before I finished him off.

I reloaded the rifle, dragged the carcass out on the creek bank, then down to the skiff. There was fresh bear sign everywhere and I wanted out of there as quickly as possible. I didn't even bother to gut him; just loaded him in the skiff and took off. I stopped about a mile down the shore, on a little gravel beach, and field-dressed the deer.

I was really reluctant to look at the hindquarter that the first bullet had passed through. When I did though, I was pleasantly surprised to find that, although the big bullet had broken the thighbone, it had stayed in one piece and exited through the flank on the other side. There was very little meat damage; just a hole through the ham and a clean exit wound. There was none of the ugly cavitation and blood-shot meat that you get with a high-velocity bullet at close range. The whole hindquarter was edible and very little meat was lost. It was some consolation for not making an instant kill, but soured me on body shots for good.

The rifle and load performed perfectly, but I was lucky that the bullet didn't hit a little farther forward. I would have had a long, dangerous search if I had gut-shot him. Little-by-little the wisdom comes.

I had the rifle for several years and it was one of my favorites. Regrettably, I sold it to a kid from Sitka who took it goat hunting in the alpine south of there. He got separated from his partner and forgot which way was home. He wandered around for several days before the Coast Guard search-and-rescue helicopter found him. He had fallen down a ravine and sprained his ankle. When he fell, he landed on the rifle and broke the stock at the wrist. He figured the gun wasn't any good without a stock, so he left it there. Too bad; it wouldn't have been hard to make a new stock for it. So it goes.

A friend of mine liked the rifle so much, he had his Mauser cut out to .338-06, a cartridge very similar to the 35 Welen. The rifle had a full-manlicher stock with a twenty-inch barrel. It turned out to be an accurate and handy rifle, and I believe he still has it.

Either of these cartridges is suitable for all North American game, if you understand their limitations. In most cases, for someone who is recoil sensitive, they are better than the bigger belted magnums. Bullet placement is still the most important factor in any type of hunting. I believe you are better off with a gun you can shoot well than one that kicks so hard that you yank the trigger and miss a vital spot. The belted magnums are more suited to shooting animals like elk at long range. On a charging grizzly at fifteen feet, the bullets give unreliable performance, and in that type of situation you don't have room for maybe.

There are two ways to get energy out of a bullet: velocity or weight. High muzzle velocity is great if the range is out past a hundred yards. However, at close range, a heavy, slow-moving bullet will penetrate more reliably and is less likely to fragment than a lightweight fast mover. When hunting for food, the slower bullet will damage less meat and carry on through so the animal will leave a good blood trail.

There are those who will disagree, but my experience bears out this notion. Keep the weight as high as possible in the biggest bore rifle you can shoot well, and keep the striking velocity below 2500 FPS. The higher the velocity, the tougher the bullet must be so it will stay in one piece and penetrate in a straight line.

Visualize a 180-grain bullet traveling at 2700 FPS and rotating at a tremendous RPM, striking a solid mass of hair, muscle and bone. It starts to deform instantly and is soon flinging pieces of itself in all directions. It starts to wobble and loses its stability rapidly. Its path becomes unpredictable and the effect of its energy becomes erratic. It might do the job sometimes, but sometimes isn't enough when your life may be at stake.

RAIN DEER

The harbor at Port Alexander is an inlet into a low peninsula that sticks out into Chatham Strait. The harbor almost cuts the peninsula off from Baranof Island, the only connection being a low neck of land between the harbor and Ship Cove in Port Conclusion. The highest point on the Peninsula is a hill that rises about 450 feet in elevation. The slopes of this knob are mostly muskeg, with a few bands of small timber scattered here and there, making the area excellent deer country. In the summer, most of the bucks cross the pass to No Name Mountain and climb up into the alpine. The does raise their fawns in the timbered areas along the shoreline until August, when they join the rest of the herd on the higher meadows. During August, September, and early October hunting on the Peninsula is pretty lean.

In late October, as the frost kills the summer foliage at higher altitudes, the deer start working their way down into the lower slopes of the mountains. Also, about this time, the rut is starting and the bucks begin staking out their territory. For the next few months the hunting is at it's best. This hill has produced a steady meat supply for the residents of Port Alexander every year since the village first appeared in the area. Because of the hunting pressure, the bucks don't usually survive to become trophy size, but they are healthy and plentiful.

A unique feature of the area that keeps the population from being depleted by human predation is that the West side of Baranof Island is seldom hunted. Because of severe weather, the area is inaccessible during much of the fall and winter. Since the herds on the outer coast have few predators, the excess population spills over onto the East side of the mountains to replace the animals taken by hunters each year.

Over the years, I spent a lot of time exploring the peninsula and got to know every deer trail and bedding area on the point. I discovered that each change in weather caused the deer to move to different feeding and bedding areas. If you knew how to approach the area the animals were using, it was fairly easy to find them. I also discovered several places where the deer would congregate as the hunting pressure increased.

The main access trail to the hill is in the northeast corner of the back lagoon and most people hunted up this trail onto a large muskeg bench about halfway up the knob. There is a mound where you could stay out of sight but look out over a large open area and watch for deer moving around in the meadow. There is better hunting to be had if you know where to look, but I liked to rest there for a few minutes and enjoy the view of the muskeg and lower Chatham Strait.

One wet, nasty October morning, I decided to take a walk, in spite of the steady drizzle that was leaking out of the low, gray overcast. It had been raining steadily for about two weeks and I was tired of lying around the house, oiling my gun and drinking coffee, while the best part of the fall was passing. I boiled up a pan of rolled oats, and after I finished eating, I suited up in rain gear and headed up the boardwalk toward the north end of town.

When I came out of the trail into the back lagoon, I noticed that the clouds were so low that the top of the small mountain was totally hidden in thick fog. I pushed my way into the dripping bushes at the beginning of the trail, then slogged up through a series of waterlogged muskegs.

The last part of the climb is a nearly vertical cliff that takes you up through a grove of cedars and into a gully with a small stream in its bottom. By the time I scrambled up the cliff, I was in the cloud. Visibility lowered to a few yards, and the air was full of a soaking mist that even made breathing difficult.

I squelched up the gully and eventually climbed out onto the mound at the edge of the big muskeg. It was like being inside a wet pearl. The whole visible world consisted of a dark green circle about fifty feet in diameter.

The West side of the mound had been hollowed out over the years by hunters using it as a stand. I lay down in the hollow and wondered why I had bothered leaving the house. Any deer with half a brain would be curled up under the branches of a cedar, chewing his cud and dreaming deer dreams.

The wet was slowly working its way inside my rain gear and I was seriously considering heading back. As I sat looking out into the fog, I realized that it was thinning slightly. I could see the blurred image of a slightly lower hump, about fifty yards down the slope to the east. While I watched, I began to be able to make out more detail. Individual bushes gradually took form out of the blurred image. I suddenly realized that there was a really big buck standing broadside to me about forty yards off, just below the crest of the next ridge! He was a dandy and as the fog thinned even more, I could see three points on each reddish-brown antler. He was completely oblivious to my presence and was just standing there looking around. He would stretch out his nose and sniff several times, then swivel his head around scanning the increasing circle of visibility that grew around him as the fog lifted.

I hunkered down in my hollow behind the mound and slid the little Ruger No. 1 into position over the top of the mound. I slipped the covers off the scope and looked at the buck through the lens. He was so close I could see water dripping off the long hairs on his neck, and the musk glands under the front corners of his eyes were clearly visible.

I seldom kill these old spawners during the rut, but this was too good a setup to let pass. I put the crosshairs on the neck, right where it joins the skull, slipped off the safety and squeezed off a shot. There was a puff of white vapor from the hot powder gas hitting the humid air, and when it cleared the buck was still standing there looking right at me.

I couldn't believe I had missed. The little Ruger was very accurate, and at forty yards it would almost put its bullets through the same hole. I opened the breach and caught the empty case. I slipped another round out of my belt and reloaded the rifle.

"Maybe I shot over him because I'm so close," I thought as I closed the breech on the fresh cartridge. I held just below the jaw line and touched off again. This time the deer trotted off about ten yards and stopped to look back at me again. I was dumbfounded. I reloaded the rifle, held on the chest behind the front shoulder, and squeezed off the third shot.

This time he bounded off about a hundred yards before stopping to look at me. I reloaded and looked at him through the scope again. The fog had lifted considerably, but I decided not to try another shot. Obviously the scope was off and I didn't want to wound him and lose him in the fog. I slid the safety into the safe position and got to my feet. When I moved, the buck raised his tail and bounced off out of sight.

I decided to go out to the beach at Judy's Cove and see if I could sight the rifle back in. I was curious about the gun, but kind of glad I hadn't killed the buck. It would have been a heck of a chore getting him to the beach, and besides he would be there to hunt another day.

I dropped down off the rim and out onto the beach in the cove. I had a rudimentary shooting bench rigged up there with a log and a couple sandbags. I rigged up a target at twenty-five paces, then fired a shot from the rest. I was using a half-sheet of plywood for a target and the bullet hit sixteen inches high and about a foot to the left. No wonder I missed!

I checked the scope mount and found that the front clamp was loose. I tightened it with the screwdriver in my Swiss Army Knife and tried her again. Two inches high and an inch to the left. I made some adjustment and moved the target out to a hundred yards.

It took several shots, but I soon had it hitting an inch high. By the time I finished, the fog had lowered again and the drizzle had turned to steady rain. I headed for home and the comfortable dryness of my shack. I was more content to wait out the wet spell, and had a story to tell over coffee at the gun shop the next morning.

I had a crack at another buck in the rain several years later, just up the hill from where I missed the one described above. I had acquired a new wife, or maybe she had acquired me. I'm not sure which. Mim loves to tramp around in the woods and also likes venison. I was working at the school that fall and got off work about 2:30 in the afternoon. We were out of meat and in the morning, as I was leaving for work, we decided she would pick me up at the back dock when school got out. We would hunt the hill east of town until dark.

It was pretty nice that morning, but as the day progressed the weather deteriorated. When Mim picked me up, the sky was overcast and it was starting to spit a mixture of rain and wet snow. She had brought rain gear, so I suited up and we headed for the back lagoon. There is an old house in the northeast corner of the lagoon and we left the skiff anchored off a gravel beach in front of the house.

As we left the beach to climb up to the muskeg bench, where I had missed the other buck a few years before, I noticed that the wind had switched from northeast to southeast. We would have it at our backs if we followed the usual route up the hill. We climbed up to the mound in the big meadow, then went west around the base of the main hill to the west.

There was a ledge that angled up the steep slope into a big muskeg west of the summit. The slope is heavily timbered, and we had quite a scramble through the wet brush up into that muskeg. We eventually came out in the open, just below the summit, but on the northwest side.

I figured we could hunt into the wind up over the top, then back down to the other muskeg and on back to the beach. It was getting dark, and the clouds were black and heavy with rain. We climbed quietly up the last slope to the top of the knob, and when we reached the crest, we lay down on a mound to look around.

About a hundred yards in front of us, across a shallow basin, there was a buck standing on a small ridge looking back at us. As we were looking at him, two other young bucks walked up out of the basin, and stopped beside the first one. I flipped the lens covers off the scope, put the crosshairs on the head of the first one we had seen, and squeezed off the shot.

When the mist cleared and I recovered from the recoil, I could see him lying on the ridge with one hind leg still kicking. The other two were still standing there looking our way. We stood up and they trotted over the ridge and disappeared.

We congratulated each other on our success as we crossed the small basin to the buck that was down. He was a nice fat two-point and would be prime eating. As we stood admiring him, Mim noticed that the other two were standing about a hundred yards away, looking back at us. I suggested she try calling them and see what they would do. I had recently taught Mim how to call a deer by making a high-pitched "eeeeee" sound and she could make a better call than I could.

Mim called and one of them started back towards us. He came about halfway before he got nervous and trotted back to his partner. She called again and they came part way toward us, then ran down a draw and disappeared.

"You should have shot another one; we could use the meat," Mim said, as I turned the buck over and started to paunch him out.

"Believe me, we have our work cut out for us just getting this one to the skiff before dark," I replied. When we finished field-dressing the deer, I looked around for the easiest route down off the hill. We were 450 feet above sea level and about a mile from the beach. It was almost dark and was snowing big, wet flakes mixed with rain. The wind had increased to about thirty knots.

The land fell away in a series of steep banks, with muskeg benches between them. The drainage was to the east, and I knew we would have to go down into the creek bottom, then back up about a hundred feet to the trail that led back to the lagoon. It was mostly muskeg, but I knew it would be no picnic.

"I'll take the deer; you carry this and keep your eyes open for bear," I said as I reloaded the rifle and handed it to Mim. I grabbed a horn and started dragging the carcass down the hill. The ground was wet and slick with the snow, which was starting to stick, but even the open country is full of gullies and brush patches that you don't see at first glance.

The only route that would take us where we wanted to go was down a gully that led to the creek bottom, about two hundred feet below the summit. As we got further down, it got narrower and full of scrub brush. The deer kept sliding into holes and Mim would have to help me pull it out. Soon we were both sweating in our rain gear and panting from exertion. It took us about twenty minutes to get down into the creek bottom and by then it was really getting dark. The snow had changed to rain and it was really coming down.

The next part of the route was uphill for about a quarter mile. It was a gut-wrenching struggle, to say the least. We didn't have time to rest much if we were going to make the beach before dark, and I didn't want to leave the deer till morning. I was afraid it would attract a bear, and it was also too warm to leave the meat with the hide on. We eventually made it up the hill and down to the beach. It was a miserable struggle and we were soaking wet with rain and sweat when we finally made it.

We pulled into the cove in front of the house and beached the skiff. Mim went and got her daughter's boyfriend to help me hang the deer on the porch. He was new in the country and had never skinned a deer, so I gave him a lesson and we soon had the hide off and the meat cleaned up.

By the time we were finished, the girls had supper ready and we told our story as we ate. I don't think the kids really appreciated the effort we had expended to bring home that much meat, but they did enjoy eating it with us over the next couple weeks.

That story reminds me of a three-point I shot at John's Bay. Fred and I had run up in his Lund skiff one clear November morning. Above John's Bay is a ridge that comes out perpendicular to the main mountain on the north side of the bay. It runs south for about a mile and ends in a gorge that drains the valley behind the ridge.

We had separated at the beach; Fred had climbed up the northeast side of the bay and I went up the edge of the gorge. There was a cliff that ran from the gorge around to the northeast. The land was heavily timbered up to the top of the cliff, then turned into a broad muskeg bowl all the way to the top of the ridge.

The rut was in full swing and as I climbed up through the cedars there was deer sign everywhere. The trail followed the edge of the gorge and was well used. There were several fresh horn rubs and a lot of old ones.

I climbed about 600 feet, then came out above the timber on the lower edge of the muskeg bowl. I skirted along the edge, staying on the brink of the gorge, until I was about 300 feet below the top of the ridge. I found a tree on a knob that gave me cover and a good view out across the muskeg bowl.

I had only been standing there about fifteen minutes when I saw a buck come out form behind a bush about 175 yards around the slope from me. I rested the rifle on a limb of the tree and fired a shot at his neck. It wasn't that hard a shot, and I don't know why I missed, but the deer never moved. I reloaded and squeezed off again, and this time the deer collapsed in his tracks with a broken neck.

I levered the empty case out of the rifle and reloaded. When the gun was safe, I walked over to the buck. He was a beaut, and the shot had taken him just back of the skull. I started gutting him out and as I worked I heard Fred's '06 boom on the hill above me. I grinned to myself and went back to work. When I had him cleaned out I picked up my rifle, grabbed a horn, and started down the hill.

I had only hunted here one other time and it had been years ago. I wasn't aware of the cliff hiding in the timber down the hill from me. The hill was steep and the ground slippery, so I just kind of let gravity do the work for me. It took about fifteen minutes to work my way down to the edge of the timber, and it wasn't long before I found myself looking down a sixty-foot vertical drop.

There was obviously no way down, so I left the deer and scouted both ways, looking for a route off the hill. After checking both directions, I found no way off the cliff. The only thing I could do was drag the carcass back up the hill and around the basin to the trail I had used on the way up the hill.

It was a formidable task. I had to go up about two hundred feet, then side-hill around the head of a small gorge that formed the beginning of the cliff. It was probably the worst piece of labor I ever performed. I thought I would have a heart attack before I got that lump of limp meat back up that hill and headed back down the right way. Even when I was going down the hill after crossing the gully at the top of the cliff, I found myself traveling perpendicular to the natural drainage most of the way. I had to drag it uphill several more times before I finally stumbled out on the gravel beach where we had left the boat.

Fred was already there, looking no worse for wear after having brought down a similar buck. He had found a ramp off the cliff around on the north end of the bowl, and said it had been easy going all the way to the beach. At least it wasn't raining.

GUNS

Over the years, I have had the privilege of hunting and experimenting with many of the calibers and rifle types that are available to the American hunter. I don't consider myself an expert, but certain patterns have emerged from my experiences.

There are two things to keep in mind while you read. The first is that most of my hunting has been done in the forests of Southeast Alaska in heavy timber and along the muskeg edges. Most game here is taken at short range in poor light conditions.

The second consideration is that much of the best deer hunting is on islands with healthy populations of Alaska brown bear. When you hunt deer in this country you need to be armed for bear. It has been my experience that a rifle/cartridge combination suitable for hunting bears is not necessarily the best choice for defending your life at close range.

At first glance, a person might think that it is necessary to hunt with the biggest, most powerful rifle you can get your hands on. There are several problems with this approach. The rifles are expensive to buy, expensive to shoot, kick too hard, and some of them can ruin a lot of meat on small deer-sized animals at close range. This dilemma is a common topic of debate and speculation among the hunters here and there is no perfect solution to it that I have discovered.

The last few years have seen an influx of new people into the area and I encounter many people with some pretty strange notions about what makes a good gun for this country. I see a lot of hunters heading for the woods carrying bolt-action rifles chambered for the belted magnum cartridges and topped with high-power scopes. Most of these rifles are great for long-range, open-country shooting and there is some of that here. The trouble is, you usually have to climb through heavily timbered areas to get to the alpine meadows, and the meat must be brought back down those same timbered slopes. A long-barreled, bolt-action rifle, with a high-magnification scope works fine for deliberate shots in open country, and at fairly long range. However, at close range in thick brush, the awkward handling qualities of these rifles may mean the difference between getting chewed or not.

Such a rifle chambered for one of the medium-bore cartridges, based on a belted case, makes a great goat or sheep gun. It works perfectly for mule deer and elk at ranges over 100 yards and works equally well on bear. However, as a close range stopping rifle, it's like trying to play baseball with a golf club.

If I want to set up a rifle for alpine hunting, I prefer a fairly short barrel, of about twenty-one inches, and a low-power variable scope. A 1.5 x 5 power is best because when you are in the timber you can set the scope on the lowest power. This gives a large field of view and is faster in close quarters.

A better sight arrangement would be a scope on mounts that allows the scope to be removed and replaced without losing its zero. A rifle equipped with one of these mounts can also have a set of iron sights zeroed in for close range. The scope can be carried separately, then installed when you get up into open country.

Imagine an enraged sow charging from fifteen feet in heavy brush. During the minute amount of time that you have to get a shot off, you must remove the lens covers, take off the safety, get a sight-picture through the scope, and fire. Good luck.... Better to click off the safety while the rifle is coming to your shoulder and fire when the sights are on the bear. If you can get a sight picture in the time allowed.

That brings up another problem with modern bolt-action rifles. They are stocked for scopes where the eyepiece is 1.5 inches above the line of the bore, or more. That means that there is little drop at the heel and the comb is high and straight. When you put iron sights on one of these rifles, they must be high enough so that the line of sight is similar to the scope. It makes the sights more vulnerable to breakage because they stick up so high, and they will probably be visible in the scope at low-power settings.

If you look at rifles that were made before scopes became popular, they had more drop at the heel and a lower comb. This was to get the line-of-sight as low as possible. It allowed the sights to be more streamlined, but more importantly made it easier to point and shoot instinctively.

Compare the stock on your shotgun to your bolt-action rifle, you will see what I mean. The shotgun is stocked for instinctive, off-hand shooting with no sights. The geometry is arranged so that when the butt is in the hollow of the shoulder and the cheek is on the comb, the gun will center its pattern where the eyes are focused at the mid-range of the load.

In the old days, the rifle stock was shaped so that when you threw it to your shoulder, you were looking down the barrel, parallel with the bore with the sights naturally aligned. Pick up an old Winchester Model 94 and throw it to your shoulder with your eyes closed. Open your eyes and you'll see what I mean.

Pick up a modern bolt gun with the scope removed and do the same thing. You will likely find you are looking at the top of the barrel, about halfway out to the muzzle. In other words, the line of the bore is at a more acute angle to the line of sight. This is necessary to compensate for bullet drop at long range, but at ten feet it is detrimental to instinctive shooting. If you try a snapshot, without time to look through the scope, you will tend to shoot high at close range.

Back in the early days, when scopes first hit the public market, most of them had a very small objective lens. The mounts were made as low as possible because the rifles were all stocked for iron sights. As scopes became more popular, and objective lenses became bigger, the mounts became higher and the factories changed the stock dimensions to suit.

Now days, about the only rifles still stocked for iron sights are the Marlin and Winchester lever-actions. Even they don't have as much drop at the heel as rifles manufactured back before W.W.II. About the only way you can get a bolt-action now that is stocked for off-hand instinctive shooting with open or peep sights is to stock it yourself. Or hire a custom stock maker to do it for you. If you can afford it. Don't miss understand. I think a good bolt gun with a scope is great out in the open, but you must be willing to risk its limitations in heavy cover.

What cartridge to chamber is for is the other half of the dilemma. Many inexperienced hunters have come to believe that bigger is better. They are convinced that if a load has three or four times more foot-pounds of energy than the animal has body weight, a hit almost anywhere will stop the animal.

Once again, it has been my experience that it's not so much how much energy you use, but how it is applied that matters. Some Eskimos at one time used the .22 Hornet to hunt polar bears. The cartridges were cheap and they could carry lots of them. They were intimately familiar with the animal's anatomy, and were skillful enough to be able to stalk to within a few yards without the bear being aware of their presence. One of those little hornet bullets through the brain will kill any bear that ever lived. The trick is to get it in there.

Hunting a bear and stopping a charge are two vastly different ball games. Sneaking up on a bear and taking him unawares, with an experienced person shooting backup, can be accomplished with rifles of quite light caliber. If the hunter is familiar with the location of the vital organs, and is able to put a bullet through one of these areas, it isn't necessary to use an elephant rifle. It is the skill of the hunter more than the power of the gun that makes the difference.

I started out with fairly small caliber rifles, then progressed up through the medium bores, and into calibers more suited for African game. I found that as the recoil increased, my ability to shoot accurately diminished. All the power in the world won't guarantee a quick, clean kill if you can't pass the bullet through a vital spot. 4000 or 5000 foot-pounds of energy might impress the heck out of your hunting partners, but the first time you shoot a chunk out of the side of a bear's head at ten feet, without penetrating the brain, or breaking the spine, you might end up wishing you had used it on yourself instead of the bear.

Some acquaintances of mine shot a three year-old brownie some years ago, with a .300 Weatherby Mag. The bear was about twenty-five yards off, and the 180-grain bullet hit it in the face below the right eye. The bear was knocked off its feet by the impact, but got right back up and vanished into the brush before they could shoot again. They had to go into the woods with their scoped rifles and look for it. Not my idea of fun!

They were lucky; the bear was young and inexperienced and didn't charge when they found it. The second shot smashed the brain for an instant kill. The first shot had blown a fist-sized chunk out of the cheek and jaw without penetrating the skull. Why? The bullet was designed to expand at ranges out to two or three hundred yards. It was too soft for close range at the high-striking velocity. It probably vaporized when it hit the cheekbone, and the tremendous energy released took the route of least resistance. It vectored off at an angle to the original line of flight. Most of the energy went off to the left, outside the bear's head.

That same bullet at half the velocity would probably have penetrated in a straight line through the left side of the skull. As it penetrated, it would have blown bone fragments up and right, through the brain. It may have even exited the head and passed on into the body cavity to damage even more tissue.

There was another incident that I heard of a few years ago where a mad sow, thinking her cubs needed protecting, charged a party of three people. She took eight shots from two .338 magnums at a range of about fifteen feet. I haven't been able to interview anyone who was involved, but I heard through reliable sources that they were shooting 250-grain Nosler Partition Bullets.

I have experimented with these bullets in several calibers and found them to be very frangible forward of the partition. The rear portion does penetrate well, but at close range and at high-striking velocities the nose is very explosive. Once that nose blows off, the bullet becomes unstable and its penetration, although deep, may be erratic. Out at normal hunting range they work very well.

I remember examining a wound in a Sitka black tail doe a few years ago that was made by a 250-grain Nosler Partition Bullet in .338 mag. The shot was fired at a range of about 25 yards at a slight downward angle. The bullet hit the base of the neck at the juncture of the right shoulder. It produced a cavity about six inches in diameter in the upper chest where the windpipe enters the body cavity.

The walls of the cavity were imbedded with particles of hair, bone fragments from the upper ribs, and tiny pieces of the bullet. The base of the bullet ended up under the skin on the back of the right ham. Excellent penetration to say the least. Unfortunately, the neck meat, both shoulders, and the rib cage were ruined. The front half of both back straps were also so bloodshot and full of bone fragments that they were also unsalvageable. The hindquarter that the base of the bullet plowed through was also a mess, to say nothing of the ruptured stomach and intestines.

The wound was gruesome and the carcass such a mess that my friend almost gave up hunting. The same shot at 150 yards after the bullet had slowed down would have probably been a clean kill with little meat damage.

The point of all of this is that the bullet must be strong enough to stay in one piece at striking velocity and retain enough of its original shape to penetrate deeply in a straight line. A bullet strong enough to stay in one piece at high-striking velocity, unfortunately, probably won't expand properly at normal hunting range. You can't have your cake and eat it too, as they say.

My philosophy is: if you're going to hunt easily-killed game in bear country, arm yourself for the worst-case-scenario and compromise on the less dangerous animal. Precise bullet placement on head and neck shots doesn't require much, if any, bullet expansion and learning to precisely place the bullet is your best weapon when your health is at stake.

Good shooting requires lots of practice. If your rifle kicks too hard, or is so expensive to shoot that you only put a few rounds through it each year, you better throttle back on the energy and find something you can shoot. More power won't replace precise bullet placement, ever. A bullet through the brain, or a broken neck, will stop any animal on earth, in its tracks!

You may have heard of an ivory hunter in Africa, early in the century, named Bell. He is said to have killed over a thousand elephants with a 7mm Mauser army rifle, using ball ammo. Once again, he was intimately familiar with the anatomy of the animal and very knowledgeable about their habits. He would walk up to within a few yards and put one of those little 175-grain non-expanding bullets through the brain, killing them instantly.

I had the privilege of reading a book that Mr. Bell wrote about his experiences. There was a chapter in it about determining your kill range. You use a target with a bulls-eye the size of the brain of the animal you're going to hunt. Start shooting at it, at about ten feet. Practice until you can hit it every time. When you can do that, you move back ten more feet, and do the same thing again. Over time, you will be able to hit the target from greater and greater distances. At any time during the process, you are perfectly aware of the maximum range at which you can hit a target of that size under any circumstances. You never attempt a shot beyond your current kill range.

If everyone followed Bell's advice, there would be a lot less wounded game each year. Fewer animals would run off to die in misery because some yahoo couldn't see past his own ego far enough to pass up shots he wasn't sure of.

A few years ago my hunting partner and I found a nice, fat, forked-horn buck that was shot dead center through both hams with a very high velocity bullet. There was a set of man tracks in the fresh snow beside the deer. We backtracked the deer and the human and found where he had jumped the buck out of its bed and took a shot off-hand, at about 75 yards. The buck was standing in plain sight, broadside to the shooter.

Making a poor shot is one thing. We have all done it from time to time, but to leave the animal to bleed to death and wasting the meat is inexcusable. It's a perfect example of the lack of morals that plague our society today. The least he could have done was shoot it again and put it out of its misery. There was only one bullet wound and it looked like he had just stood there watching it bleed out, then walked away.

Over the years, I have come up with a rule of thumb about bullets and loads for this type of hunting. It goes something like this.

"Use the heaviest bullet available in the caliber you choose, and keep the striking velocity well below 2500 feet per second."

The closer to 2500 fps the striking velocity is, the tougher the bullet needs to be. As for energy, a couple thousand foot-pounds is adequate for anything in North America, if applied correctly. I'm referring to striking energy, not muzzle energy.

I also tend to favor a fairly large diameter bullet. When the bore diameter is above thirty-five caliber, it is easier to find bullets tough enough to hold together and penetrate deeply at very close range.

One of my favorite rifles over the years has been a Marlin lever-action, chambered for 45-70. I bought the first one years ago when Marlin first came out with the model 1895 SS. I used that one so much that I pretty much wore it out. I have recently bought a new one and am sad to say that Marlin, in trying to dress up the rifle and keep manufacturing costs down, has given up some quality. It is still a good rifle, though, and with a little tinkering it is still my favorite.

I have experimented with many powder and bullet combinations over the years. By hand loading you can significantly increase the power of the 45-70 cartridge. You can get up in the 3000 foot-pound range if you can stand the recoil. However I have gradually reduced my loads back to about the same as the standard factory rounds. At close range, a 450-grain slug at about 1200-1400 fps will shoot through the biggest bear in the country. The wound channel won't be very large in diameter, but the bullet will penetrate deeply in a fairly straight line. The rifle is fairly pleasant to shoot with factory cartridges, and they are not so expensive that you can't afford to practice.

The Marlin lever-actions are about the only rifle you can buy anymore that are drilled and tapped for a receiver sight. Lyman and Williams both manufacture well-made peep sights for these rifles and I highly recommend them. I usually sight in with the smallest aperture I can get my hands on, then carry it in my pocket while hunting. At ranges of fifty yards or less, the large hole works fine, and it is easy to see through it in poor light. All you have to do on a quick shot are look through the hole in the back sight and put the front bead on the spot you want to hit. If I want to make a longer shot where I have a rest and plenty of time, I screw the aperture back in and it extends the accurate range to about 100 yards.

Another advantage of these rifles is the tubular magazine. You can reload the magazine without opening the breech of the rifle. Whenever I shoot a deer, I always lever another cartridge into the chamber and set the hammer on half cock. When there is a fresh shell in the chamber, I shove another one into the magazine to replace the one I just fired. That leaves five cartridges in the rifle while I gut and drag out the deer. The gun also holds four shells in the magazine; a magnum bolt-action only holds three.

I usually hunt alone, so I carry a round in the chamber with the hammer on half cock. If I need to make a quick shot, I can ear the hammer back as the rifle comes up and fire when the sights are aligned. It's a heck of a lot faster than scope covers off, safety off, then trying to find the bear in the lens of the scope. What if you forget to turn the power back to the lowest magnification?

THE END

Afterword

As a young man I did not see the animals I hunted as fellow creatures. They were a commodity to be harvested and there was a certain machismo connected with hunting prowess that I indulged in. As time passed I began to see them more as fellow travelers through the mystery of life and it became difficult to justify killing them. I struggled with these feelings of compassion for several years, and even stopped hunting for a time.

Wandering in the forest for thirty years changed me in some subtle way. The natural world tolerated my ignorance, fed me when I was hungry, and led me to new levels of understanding of myself and the world around me. The cells in my body became one with the flesh of the animals and plants that nourished me, and the water of the streams flowed in my veins. I began to stop seeing myself as separate from the rest of nature. The illusion of superiority faded and was replaced with a sense of belonging. The notion that I had a right to possess anything I could gather onto myself was replaced with an understanding that the taking of life to meet your needs is a sacred privilege.

This country has changed much in the last thirty years. Many of the places described have been heavily logged and will never be the same again. Industrial tourism is sweeping through the region and wilderness has become a commodity. There is so much increase in demand for access, that the U.S. Forest Service is working on a plan to determine how many people can visit each area per year.

The mountains are still there, the rivers still flow, and deer bears and other critters still roam in what is left of the forest, but the wild is disappearing from the wilderness.

0-595-21263-8

Printed in the United States
785700003B